What's the

BIG IDEA?

What's the

BIG IDEA?

Question-Driven Units to Motivate

Reading, Writing, and Thinking

JIM BURKE

HEINEMANN
Portsmouth, NH

Heinemann
361 Hanover Street
Portsmouth, NH 03801–3912
www.heinemann.com

Offices and agents throughout the world

The author and publisher wish to thank those who have generously given permission to reprint borrowed material:

"Types of Questions" from *Academic Workout: Reading and Language Arts* by Timothy Rasinski and Jim Burke. Copyright © 2007 by First Choice Education Group. Published by Curriculum Associates, Inc. Reprinted by permission of the publisher.

Screenshot from www.schoolloop.com. Reprinted by permission of School Loop, Inc.

Red Cross campaign advertisement. Reprinted by permission of the American Red Cross.

"The Big Questions" from the *McDougal Littell Literature Series* by Janet Allen, Arthur N. Applebee, and Jim Burke. Copyright © 2007. Published by Holt McDougal, a division of Houghton Mifflin Company. Reprinted by permission of the publisher.

Excerpt from *The Teacher's Daybook, 2009–2010* by Jim Burke. Copyright © 2009 by Jim Burke. Published by Heinemann. Reprinted by permission of the publisher.

Library of Congress Cataloging-in-Publication Data
Burke, Jim.
    What's the big idea? : question-driven units to motivate reading, writing, and thinking / Jim Burke.
        p. cm.
        Includes bibliographical references and index.
        ISBN-13: 978-0-325-02157-7
        ISBN-10: 0-325-02157-0
        1. Language arts (Secondary).   2. Literature—Study and teaching (Secondary).
    3. Questioning.   I. Title: Question-driven units to motivate reading, writing, and thinking.
LB1631.B7739 2010
428.0071'2—dc22   2009039569

Editor: Lisa Luedeke
Production: Abigail M. Heim
Typesetter: Kim Arney
Interior and cover design: Lisa A. Fowler
Back cover photograph: Sarah Finnegan
Manufacturing: Steve Bernier

Printed in the United States of America on acid-free paper

14   13   12   11   10   VP   2   3   4   5

Whoever said a dictionary definition is the most realistic answer to the meaning of something? I am not doubting the dictionary. I just find myself questioning what is absolute. I guess I am grateful for this because I feel that the ability to ask a question has been lost; whether it is asking someone what their favorite color is, to understanding where you come from. . . . I don't understand the fear of speaking and understanding. Because I believe being able to grasp and understand something is the key to learning.

—Sara Buckingham, blog from Jim Burke's senior English class

Jim Burke is always in the midst of dialogue—with colleagues in schools, with his students, with the larger professional community. That is how I first met him, with an emailed question about something he was writing, prompted by something I had written. And though we've gone on to become friends and colleagues, that first electronic interchange made a lasting impression, of someone at the center of things, asking good questions and seeking answers anywhere he can find them.

And now in this book, Jim shows us how that same propensity to ask interesting questions can and should lie at the heart of the curriculum—whether dealing with freshmen beginning their high school careers with some uncertainty and trepidation, or seniors who need a special challenge to stay engaged with anything other than their future lives in the closing weeks of their final semester. (Or indeed, the adult readers of this book, who are challenged with questions to guide their reading in an appended discussion guide.)

What's the Big Idea?, Jim asks in his title, and then goes on to show us how a focus on big ideas and enduring questions can, over extended periods of time, add depth and rigor to the curriculum, while simultaneously increasing student interest and engagement. Indeed, when we don't ask good questions, ones that provoke multiple perspectives and demand a careful mustering of argument, can we blame students when they become bored and disinterested?

Many people have written about how theory (or research) relates to practice; Jim is one of those rare professionals who lives the relationship. His book is rich with insights from other scholars and teachers, woven together in a convincing web of argument and insight. But the book is just as rich in classroom experience, using the wisdom of the expert practitioner to focus his arguments in the lives of his students—in all their richness and complexity. It is a perfect example of what I have elsewhere called "principled practice," in which a master teacher's repertoire is guided by a deep understanding of important principles of effective teaching and learning.

Part of Jim's wisdom is recognizing that the devil is in the details, and as the chapters in this book unfold he pays close attention to the many demands any teacher must juggle. How to orient urban kids toward the landscape and people in *Of Mice and Men* (try Google Earth, and follow up with Dorothy Lange photos from the Internet); how to read all the postings from online discussion groups with thirty-five students in a class (don't; just scan the discussion and step in when a group is getting off track or lost); how to be sure that you are paying attention to all the skills that students will need to learn (use backward design, with his one-page Academic Essentials chart to monitor what has been covered); how to make students "test wise" without extended test prep (have students design and discuss their own questions).

In my own work with teachers, the issues Jim tackles here are among the most difficult. For many teachers, it is much easier to rethink one lesson or lesson sequence at a time than it is to rethink a full unit . . . and it is even harder to tie the unit together around an extended exploration of a question that matters. (It is also much easier to explore a theme with a series of activities unrelated to one another, which is why thematic teaching sometimes falls flat.) Jim's book does not make it *easy* to rethink a curriculum—indeed he is careful to chronicle the many different things a teacher has to consider—but it does make it seem *possible*. And this sense of possibility is greatly enhanced by the inclusion of a wide variety of teaching materials in reproducible format—everything from setting up summer reading assignments to traditional essays to multimedia presentations—together with extended examples of the work that students produced in response.

It is impossible to leave Jim's book saying, "but kids can't really do that," and equally hard to leave it wondering just where to start, because Jim gives teachers everything they need to begin this journey on their own.

—Arthur Applebee

Every book you write is the work of many hands and all the minds you met along the way, each of which shaped your thinking and thus the book. This is especially true for this one, for it is not the book I set out to write. Thus I am most grateful for my editor, Lisa Luedeke, who looked through all that I sent her and saw within it a better book, a more important idea that she helped me to see one day over lunch at NCTE. Not only did Lisa discover within my pages a better book, but she also worked for two years to help me get it just right. We worked through this book several times, refining the ideas, then taking them back into the classroom to improve them. It was truly a collaborative effort, though any flaws you may find here are entirely my own and evidence that there is yet still more for me to learn. Although we have worked together on a few other books, this marks the first book I have written with Lisa's editorial guidance and mentoring from start to finish. I am so grateful for her patient wisdom and steady encouragement and look forward to all future projects with her.

In addition to Lisa, I must thank others at Heinemann, especially Maura Sullivan, Kate Montgomery, Wendy Murray, and Lesa Scott for the time they took to advise me on not only this book but also my future ones. This book marks the beginning of a new direction of sorts for me as a writer: fewer books, more thoroughly researched, more carefully anchored in classroom instruction with a greater emphasis on differentiation due to the range of kids I now teach. I spent more time researching, writing, and rewriting this book than perhaps any other I have written so far and now offer it to you with great pride and satisfaction. Also at Heinemann are those who turned my messy pages into the book you hold: Abby Heim, Lisa Fowler, Eric Chalek, Marilyn Rash, Stephanie Turner, Nicole Russell, and Steve Bernier.

Many thanks to Roderick Spelman at Holt McDougal Harcourt (and to HMH itself) for securing permission to include the Big Questions here. They are a tremendous gift to teachers and a substantial addition to this book. Also, many thanks to the Anti-Defamation League for permission to include their Pyramid of

Hate. Additional thanks to Linda Christensen for permission to include her bystander assignment (and her contributions to our field in general).

As the pages will show, my greatest debt is and always will be to my students. Here you see us at work over the course of extended units, wrestling with big ideas, doing the great work of English over the course of a year. Even though I wrote this book based on the work of students in my CP freshman and AP Lit classes from one year, I had time to test these same ideas out and revise them in light of new learning in the subsequent year. This extended time also had the added benefit of allowing me to test the validity and reliability of the material in this book: Did it work again, with different kids? The answer is a resounding yes; perhaps as important, I shared many of these ideas with other teachers through workshops and at school and found the materials and concepts here worked as well—sometimes even better!—in others' hands as they did in my own.

At Burlingame High School, where I have now taught for eighteen years, I must thank my colleagues Tim Larkin, Shane Karshan, and Diane McClain for their influence on my ideas shared here and teaching in general. Special thanks, however, goes to Morgan Hallabrin, with whom I collaborate on nearly all my classes (and who took over the ACCESS program and has continued to improve on that model and help those kids). Our daily conversations provide me with my own personal think tank about English, and for her insights and ideas I am truly grateful. I also want to thank the whole English department at Burlingame High School; no teacher ever had a more supportive, enjoyable bunch of colleagues to work with.

Finally, I must thank my wife, Susan, for her continued support and encouragement. Our three wonderful kids—Evan, Whitman, and Nora—play increasingly important and influential roles in my writing and thinking about teaching as I listen to and talk with them about their own ideas and experiences in school. Without the support of my wife and children, no books are possible. They are the "Big Ideas" in my daily life.

Jim Burke
www.englishcompanion.com

What's the
BIG IDEA?

Why Do Questions Matter in Curriculum?

An Introduction

Students enter school as question marks and graduate as periods.

—NEAL POSTMAN

The use of questions as a curricular framework is, of course, not new. Socrates used it, asking questions such as "What is virtue?" "What is justice?" and "What is good?" (Phillips 2004). In *Socratic Circles: Fostering Critical and Creative Thinking in Middle and High School,* Matt Copeland (2005) summarizes "Socratic questioning" as a means of using

> . . . questioning to bring forward already held ideas in the students' minds, to make them more aware and cognizant of the learning and understanding that has already occurred. . . . Socratic questioning is a systematic process for examining the ideas, questions, and answers that form the basis of human belief. It involves recognizing that all new understanding is linked to prior understanding, that thought itself is a continuous thread woven through our lives rather than isolated sets of questions and answers. (8)

Picking up on this notion of questions and Socratic inquiry, Ted Sizer (1985) called for instruction to be organized around "essential questions" that students would use to understand the big ideas in a course; that is, the ideas they would explore and grapple with through discussions, written responses, and ongoing investigations and research—all of which might culminate in a paper, a presentation, or some appropriate project or artifact. Sizer's approach, which begins with the belief that every student can think critically and do serious academic work, is described in the following passage:

> But where might an individual teacher begin? The starting point, as Grant Wiggins argues, is to "organize courses not around 'answers' but around questions and problems to which 'content' represents answers." Such "essential questions," as they are known, are an important ingredient of curriculum reform . . . . On every level, the "essential question" should shape the way students learn to think critically for themselves.
>
> At Central Park East Secondary School in New York City, for example, the entire curriculum is focused on getting students to ask and answer questions like these: "From whose viewpoint are we seeing or reading or hearing? How do we know what we know? How are things, events, and people connected to each other? What in this idea is new and what [is] old? Why does this matter?" (Cushman 1989, 2)

Increasingly scripted, controlled curriculum has driven the instruction of many for some years now; results are clear: students show no clear gains in enduring knowledge or the deeper cognitive skills demanded by the workplace as a result of such test-driven curriculum. Throughout this book, I offer examples of questions—and lessons, units, and courses organized around those questions— you can use in your own classroom to increase engagement, understanding, and retention.

It is such generative thinking (Langer 2002) that Marzano, Pickering, and Pollock (2001) found in effective instruction in their research, concluding that "'higher-level' questions produce deeper learning than 'lower-level' questions" (113), especially when used "*before* a learning experience to establish a 'mental set' with which students process the learning experience" (114). Summing up the research on questions as they relate to reading comprehension and instruction

in the "dialogic classroom," Nystrand (2006) reported that "discussion-based instruction, in the context of high academic demands, significantly enhanced literature achievement and reading comprehension" (400).

Nystrand continues: "What counts as knowledge and understanding in any given classroom is largely shaped by the questions teachers ask, how they respond to their students, and how they structure small-group and other pedagogical activities" (400). Looking further into questions and their use to improve classroom discourse and student learning, Nystrand has

> . . . found that such discourse "moves" as authentic (open-ended) questions and uptake (follow-up questions) significantly enhanced the probability of both discussion and dialogic "spells" (phases of classroom discourse intermediate between recitation and open discussion characterized by clusters of student questions). Student questions had the strongest effect of all . . . . [Nystrand also found that] authentic teacher questions and uptake, to the extent that they were used, suppressed potentially negative effects of macro variables such as track, SES, race, and ethnicity; this finding clarifies the critical importance of high-quality classroom discourse in English language arts instruction. (403)

Questions are the Swiss Army knife of an active, disciplined mind trying to understand texts or concepts and communicate that understanding to others. Some questions, like the biggest knife blade, do most of the work; other questions, similar to the corkscrew or leather punch, are more specialized, used only on rare occasions but essential when needed. It would be nice if we could just give each student such a set of cognitive tools and send them into the world; the truth, however, is that they need not only the questions themselves but the knowledge of which ones to ask and how and when to ask them.

> **?** *Questions are the Swiss Army knife of an active, disciplined mind trying to understand texts or concepts and communicate that understanding to others.*

To thrive as students in a "flat world" (Friedman 2006), as employees during the "Conceptual Age" (Pink 2006), and as citizens in a "post-American world" (Zakaria 2008), students need an intellectual flexibility that allows them to generate a range of questions as well as possible answers, to evaluate a subject from multiple perspectives. Costa and Ballick (2000) call such mental capacities "habits of mind"—a term the

California State University (ICAS) also applied in its report on academic success (p. 8) in which they responded to the question, "What constitutes academic literacy?" by saying:

> The dispositions and habits of mind that enable students to enter the ongoing conversations appropriate to college thinking, reading, writing, and speaking are interrelated and multi-tiered. Students should be aware of the various logical, emotional, and personal appeals used in argument; additionally, they need skills enabling them to define, summarize, detail, explain, evaluate, compare/contrast, and analyze. Students should also have a fundamental understanding of audience, tone, language usage, and rhetorical strategies to navigate appropriately in various disciplines.
>
> Our study informs our conclusions about the complex nature of academic literacy. Competencies in reading, writing, listening, speaking, and in the use of technology . . . presuppose the intellectual dispositions valued by the community college, CSU, and UC faculty who teach first-year students and participated in our study. They tell us, and our experience confirms, that the following intellectual habits of mind are important for students' success. The percentages noted indicate the portion of faculty who identified the following as "important to very important" or "somewhat to very essential" in their classes and within their academic discipline. College and university students should be able to engage in the following broad intellectual practices:
>
> - exhibit curiosity (80%)
> - experiment with new ideas (79%)
> - see other points of view (77%)
> - challenge their own beliefs (77%)
> - engage in intellectual discussions (74%)
> - ask provocative questions (73%)
> - generate hypotheses (72%)
> - exhibit respect for other viewpoints (71%)
> - read with awareness of self and others (68%)

Central to each of these habits, though not always visible, is the ability to ask effective questions—some obvious and intuitive, others more sophisticated—

that we must teach our students how to formulate and use. Academic discourse is not, for most students, a natural, familiar language; rather, it is one that uses its own conventions and vernacular, one that requires students to cultivate a "disciplined mind" (Gardner 2006) if they are to graduate prepared to meet the demands of the workplace and the university. The *Academic Literacy* report, focusing on these same concerns about critical thinking, continues:

> Generally, college faculty who participated in our study have concerns about the habits of mind of their first-year students. Among the narrative comments, we find assertions that students "are more diligent than in the past, but less able to tackle difficult questions, and much less curious"; "students today seem unwilling to engage in the hard work of thinking, analyzing, unless it is directed to their most immediate interests"; students "overemphasize the skill dimension of the discipline, and ignore the communication dimension," and, regrettably, "they do not know how to seek help and demand attention."
>
> Faculty expect students to have an appetite to experiment with new ideas, challenge their own beliefs, seek other points of view, and contribute to intellectual discussions, all of which demand increasingly astute critical thinking skills.

Critical Thinking: The Cornerstone of Success

Critical thinking generally refers to a set of cognitive habits and processes. Thus, critical thinkers recursively engage in probative questioning, rigorous analysis, and imaginative synthesis and evaluation of ideas. Such thinking ability can be acquired through effort and instruction and is crucial to success in all academic disciplines.

Although the 9–12 California English Language Arts Content Standards call for students to identify, describe, compare/contrast, trace, explain, analyze, interpret, and evaluate, often students do not build on these abilities toward higher-order critical thinking skills. Forty percent of our study respondents indicated that their students' "ability to tackle complex, analytical work" has declined over the course of their teaching years, a figure that rises dramatically with faculty's length of service. The responses do not suggest the causes of such perceptions; but whatever those causes might be, educators want to avoid, as one faculty notes, "thought processes [that] seem shallow, like 'sound

bytes.'" While such sound bytes may characterize aspects of the culture at large, they do not characterize the academic culture, which prizes reflective habits of mind regarding critical reading, writing, listening, and thinking.

As one respondent puts it, "If [students] can't write well, I don't see evidence that they can think well." Analytical thinking must be taught, and students must be encouraged to apply those analytical abilities to their own endeavors as well as to the work of others. Students whose abilities in critical reading and think-ing enable them to grasp an argument in another's text can construct argu-ments in their own essays. Those who question the text will be more likely to question their own claims. Frequent exposure to a variety of rhetorical strate-gies in their reading empowers students to experiment with and develop their own rhetorical strategies as writers. (ICAS 2000)

New concerns about academic readiness and engagement have emerged in various books such as *Distracted* (Jackson 2008); *The Path to Purpose* (Damon 2008); and Mark Bauerlein's detailed criticism, *The Dumbest Generation: How the Digital Age Stupefies Young Americans and Jeopardizes Our Future* (2008). Bauer-line, whose book includes those critiques offered in the other books, sums up his argument thus:

> The Dumbest Generation cares little for history books, civic principles, foreign affairs, comparative religions, and serious media and art, and it knows less. Ca-reening through their formative years, they don't catch the knowledge bug, and *tradition* might as well be a foreign word. Other things monopolize their atten-tion—the allure of screens, peer absorption, career goals. They are latter day Rip Van Winkles, sleeping through the movements of culture and events of his-tory, preferring the company of peers to great books and powerful ideas and momentous happenings. From their ranks will emerge few minds knowledge-able and interested enough to study, explain, and dispute the place and mean-ing of our nation. (234)

Some will argue that such high expectations are unreasonable, even impos-sible. I understand such concerns, yet I go to work each day in a district, as more and more teachers throughout the country do, that has made the state university entrance requirements our district's graduation requirements, believing as Adler (1982) says, that "the education for the best is the best education for all" (6).

Moreover, in an attempt to inspire more students to challenge themselves at the highest levels, my district, as many around the country have also done, instituted an open enrollment policy that says anyone who wants to take Advanced Placement courses can do so. Thus teachers are challenged to teach *all* students at a higher level, sometimes taking a rather circuitous route to get there but guided by the belief that students can get there if they follow our lead. In the subsequent units, I try to illustrate how such high standards can be reached in both College Prep and Advanced Placement courses, with those at both ends of the spectrum in each class, and all those in between.

? *Direct and guided instruction in formulating and using questions helps demystify what highly effective students do.*

As is often, though not always, the case, successful readers, writers, and thinkers have learned to ask certain questions other students have not; direct and guided instruction in formulating and using these questions to generate, comprehend, analyze, and elaborate begins to demystify what those highly effective students do and thus builds in the others a sense of emerging confidence that this is work they *can* do once they learn how. As Adler (1982) wrote:

> All genuine learning is active, not passive. It involves the use of the mind, not just memory. It is a process of discovery in which the student is the main agent, not the teacher. How does a teacher aid discovery and elicit the activity of the student's mind? By inviting and entertaining questions, by encouraging and sustaining inquiry, by supervising helpfully a wide variety of exercises and drills, by leading discussions, by giving examinations that arouse constructive responses, not just the making of check marks on printed forms. (50)

And it *is* work they must learn to do, for their—and our—economic success depends on it as a growing chorus is quick to remind us. Many in the workplace express their concerns about the need for intellectual abilities because they have a direct bearing on productivity, innovation, and overall success in the marketplace. As the National Council on Education and the Economy (NCEE) found in its landmark report, *Tough Choices or Tough Times* (2007), ours is a "world in which a very high level of preparation in reading, writing, speaking, mathematics, science, literature, history, and the arts will be an indispensible foundation for everything that comes after for most members of the workforce" (xviii).

Increasingly, it is not the threat that jobs will be sent overseas that worries observers (Friedman 2006; NCEE 2007; Pink 2006) but that such jobs will be done by machines, even white-collar jobs, such as an accountant, once thought safe. Thus, as the NCEE report goes on to say:

> Strong skills in English, mathematics, technology, and science, as well as literature, history, and the arts will be essential for many; beyond this, candidates will have to be comfortable with ideas and abstractions, good at both analysis and synthesis, creative and innovative, self-disciplined and well-organized, able to learn very quickly and work well as a member of a team and have the flexibility to adapt to frequent changes in the labor market as the shifts in the economy become ever faster and more dramatic. (xix)

Pink (2006) calls the current era the "Conceptual Age," contrasting it with previous eras—the Industrial, when people were factory workers; the Information Age, during which people were knowledge workers—to argue that America must now, if we are to maintain our place in the world, become "a society of creators and emphathizers, of pattern recognizers and meaning makers" (50). Fareed Zakaria (2008) places Pink's argument in a larger, more global context. Of America's educational system, he writes:

> While the American system is too lax on rigor and memorization—whether in math or poetry—it is much better at developing the critical faculties of the mind, which is what you need to succeed in life. Other educational systems teach you to take tests; the American system teaches you to think. (193)

As Zakaria himself acknowledges, however, not all students are in schools where they are taught to think. Indeed, too often underachieving students have no opportunity to ask or respond to questions that would connect school to their lives outside; instead, these disaffected students are too often working to develop skills through a curriculum that offers them no chance to ask the questions that they desperately need answers to. Jackson and Cooper (2007) argue that teachers must

> . . . switch their instruction focus from *what must be taught* to *what kinds of teaching will maximize learning*. Maximizing learning to reverse underachievement in literacy for our adolescents requires a change in the very definition of literacy itself; we must embrace a definition of literacy that:

- fosters engagement of behaviors vital to adolescents (making connections, inquiring, giving personal perspective, critically evaluating situations)
- incorporates authentic literacy—literacy relevant to students; and
- recognizes the critical role of a student's frame of reference in literacy development, enabling them to feel smart again. (248)

Thomas Friedman outlines his solution to these problems of disengagement and inequity, going to the heart of this book and its main premise about teaching: "Nobody works harder at learning than a curious kid" (2006, 304). Friedman offers his own equation to sum up his premise:

> I have concluded that in a flat world, IQ—intelligence quotient—still matters, but CQ and PQ—curiosity quotient and passion quotient—matter even more . . . . Give me a kid with a passion to learn and a curiosity to discover and I will take him or her over a less passionate kid with a high IQ every day of the week. Because curious, passionate kids are self-educators and self-motivators. (304)

While the concerns of both the university and the workplace are important, another, equally urgent issue has emerged, the one Jackson and Cooper allude to earlier: the existential crisis many young people are experiencing. As Figure 1.12 shows, students today are, as Rilke said, "living the questions" and it is often a difficult experience, even for those who appear to have found a purpose.

Damon (2008) conducted a major study of purpose and found that

> . . . only about one in five young people in the 12–22 year age range express a clear vision of where they want to go, what they want to accomplish in life, and why. The largest portion of those [they] interviewed—almost 60 percent—may have engaged in some potentially purposeful activities, or they may have developed some vague aspirations; but they do not have any real commitment to such activities or any realistic commitment to such activities or any realistic plans for pursuing their aspirations. (8)

Damon, painting a troubling picture of today's youth that extends, according to his research, well beyond the United States, identifies the

> . . . most pervasive problem of the day [as] a sense of emptiness that has ensnared many young people in long periods of drift during a time in their lives

when they should be defining their aspirations and making progress toward their fulfillment. For too many young people today, apathy and anxiety have become the dominant moods, and disengagement or even cynicism has replaced the natural hopefulness of youth. (xii)

Echoing some of Friedman's previous sentiment about the role of curiosity and passion, Damon says the message that

. . . young people do best when they are challenged to strive, to achieve, to serve . . . fails to address the most essential question of all: *For what purpose*? Or, in a word, *Why*? For young people, this concern means starting to ask— and answer—questions such as: What do I hope to accomplish with all my efforts, with all the striving that I am expected to do? What are the higher goals that give these efforts meaning? What matters to me; and why should it matter? What is my ultimate concern in life? Unless we make such questions a central part of our conversations with young people, we can do little but sit back and watch while they wander into a sea of confusion, drift, self-doubt, and anxiety—feelings that too often arise when work and striving are unaccompanied by a sense of purpose. (xii)

> **?** *There are some very important existential questions students must have occasion to ask if they are to engage with their studies and develop essential comprehension and other academic skills.*

Although no one thing can ever be the solution to all problems, this book demonstrates the ways in which questions can address the concerns just outlined and develop in our students the mental acuity and fluency necessary to succeed in school and at work, as well as to achieve a sense of purpose in their personal lives.

As Damon illustrates and stresses, there are some very important existential questions students must have occasion to ask if they are to engage with their studies; Jackson and Cooper, in their research of underachieving students, arrived at the same conclusion, as have others who have investigated engagement and motivation (Smith and Wilhelm 2002; Guthrie and Wigfield 1997; Intrator 2005). Such questions, as well as others they must learn to ask, not only address existential needs but also develop essential comprehension and other academic skills needed to enter into the discussion.

All of the preceding issues and concerns seem to come together in the work of Howard Gardner, most notably his book *Five Minds for the Future* (2006), a

book in which he asserts that there are five "minds" "that are particularly at a premium in the world today and will be even more so tomorrow" (4). Gardner posits that the five minds are essential to our success and, thus, offer a crucial guide to teachers who seek to prepare their students to live in the world:

- The *disciplined mind* has mastered at least one way of thinking—a distinctive mode of cognition that characterizes a specific scholarly discipline, craft, or profession . . . [and] knows how to work steadily over time to improve skill and understanding.

- The *synthesizing mind* takes information from disparate sources, understands and evaluates that information objectively, and puts it together in ways that make sense to the synthesizer and also to [an]other person.

- The *creating mind* breaks new ground. It puts forth new ideas, poses unfamiliar questions, conjures up fresh ways of thinking, arrives at unexpected answers.

- The *respectful mind* notes and welcomes differences between human individuals and between human groups, tries to understand these "others," and seeks to work effectively with them.

- The *ethical mind* ponders the nature of one's work and the needs and desires of the society in which one lives. This mind conceptualizes how workers can serve purposes beyond self-interest and how citizens can work unselfishly to improve the lot of all. (3)

The assignments and examples included in this book reflect the kind of teaching that honors and, more importantly, develops these different minds while at the same time addressing the existential needs of students who must, if they are to succeed, master the content outlined in the state standards. Questions are the engine in such a classroom, for when students' instruction is organized around meaningful, clear questions, they understand better, remember longer, and engage much more deeply and for greater periods of time.

Returning to our earlier analogy of questions as a Swiss Army knife, we might say that each feature of the knife represents a different type of question. Some questions are intended to analyze and evaluate; others work best to help us make different types of connections; and still other questions are more reflective, raising philosophical and ethical as well as personal issues important to students' lives. Whatever their purpose, regardless of their particular type, questions help direct

our thinking and, in this instance, our teaching. Inherent in the very word is a sense of direction, an end toward which all our energies are directed: *quest*-ion. This purposeful aspect is perhaps most evident in one of the most fundamental uses of the question—the scientific method:

- Ask a question.
- Conduct background research.
- Construct an hypothesis.
- Test your hypothesis through research.
- Analyze your data and draw a conclusion.
- Communicate your results.

The Art of Teaching Questions

As students learn these questions—or, in some instances, sets of questions—they develop an independence of mind—an intellectual facility that serves them well whether reading or writing, researching or presenting, evaluating or analyzing, comparing or contrasting. Yet such questions must be taught to them; how to do this? Figure 1 shows a handout I created to use in both my freshman college prep English class and AP Literature class. Note several features of the handout, which is designed to teach students to ask not only different types of questions but effective questions (thus the examples and the qualities listed).

A full-size version of this handout, customizable and reproducible, is available at www. heinemann.com.

It is designed to be used initially as either an overhead, which allows us to work on these questions collaboratively, or a hard copy so that they can work on it individually or in groups. In addition, it includes the qualities of each type of question, and thus functions as a checklist for students to consult when creating their own questions; this list also serves as a rubric, allowing my students and me to check questions we are discussing against the descriptors. Also important, for students working at any level, are the examples. These provide a subtle means of differentiating the class as they provide examples of a range of questions, some of which are more sophisticated than others. Finally, in addition to providing a space for students to write their questions, it demands not only response (i.e., "write the answer"), but citation (i.e., "cite the page number") and analysis (i.e., "explain its importance").

Types of Questions

Directions: After reading the assigned text, create one of each type of question, accompanied by the additional information requested. Be prepared to contribute these questions to class discussion with evidence from the assigned text.

1. Factual Question • Is verifiable—answers found on the page. • Responds to questions: *who, what, when, where, how?* • Takes the reader *into* the text. *Examples* • Who does Romeo kill? • What does everyone in the book think Ultima is? • Where does George tell Lennie to go if he gets in trouble again? • When is the story set?	Write *your* factual question here: Write the answer, cite the page number, and explain its importance below.
2. Inductive Question • Is verifiable—answers found *in* the text, based on details and examples. • Responds to questions: *why, how,* and *so what?* • Takes readers *through* the text, allowing them to evaluate and interpret evidence from the visual, spoken, or written text. *Examples* • Why does George continue to care for Lennie after all the trouble he causes? • How does O'Brien convey his attitude toward the war in this story? • Why does Hamlet treat Ophelia as he does? • How does Ralph's relationship with the others change by the end of the story?	Write *your* inductive question here: Write the answer, provide the examples, and explain its importance below.
3. Analytical Question • Connects the text to other texts, ideas, or situations through analysis. • Responds to questions: *How are these similar, different, related?* • Takes readers *beyond* the text, allowing them to analyze the relationship between this text and other texts, ideas, events, or situations. *Examples* • How is *Frankenstein* similar to certain modern problems we face today? • In what ways are *The Plague* and *Blindness* similar and different? • What does *Lord of the Flies* tell us about human nature?	Write *your* analytical question here: Write the answer, provide the examples, and explain its importance below.

Figure 1 Types of Questions handout for creating effective questions

In a college prep English class, especially when introducing such strategies the first time, I would give each student a hardcopy, place the same sheet on the overhead, and focus on one type of question at a time. I might, for example, use this handout when students are reading their independent reading books or a selection from the Holt McDougal textbook we use, blocking out all but the "Factual Question" section on the overhead. After a brief discussion about what constitutes a fact—during which I make provocative statements like, "The Lakers are the greatest team of all time—is that a fact?" which I know *some* boys will engage with—I go over the examples provided on the handout, asking them what makes these factual questions. Following a brief discussion, during which I will correct or clarify any misconceptions, I create a sample based on my own reading (I read my own book while they read theirs during silent reading time). Again, we discuss my question, how I might answer it, and what makes it important.

It is this last step—"evaluate its importance"—that is the most difficult for students, especially inexperienced readers. They often confuse importance to *them* with importance to the *story*, believing that because they had a similar experience it is important, instead of understanding that certain details are essential to the story's structure. This is something I often must take extra time to clarify usually by asking students, "How do you determine if something is important to the text?" When someone says something like, "If you took it out it would be a completely different story," I know we are on the right track because this gives them a useful question to evaluate importance and gives us one we can use as a class to check our thinking.

> **?** *We have a three-step process to follow for most instruction: I do it (teacher models); we do it (create one together); they do it (independently).*

After they have seen me use the handout, it is time for us to try one together. Using whatever common text we are reading at that time (for example, *Of Mice and Men*), we create some sample factual questions together, evaluating them according to the criteria outlined on the handout to determine *if* they are factual questions and how important they are. After successfully developing some questions together, I turn them loose to create their own, after which they must check with each other to evaluate them, nominating from their group the best question so that we can further discuss it.

Thus we have a three-step process to follow for most instruction: I do it (teacher models); we do it (create one together); they do it (independently). Once

they have mastered the chosen type of question (in this case, the factual question), we move on to learn about the other types in subsequent days or weeks according to the class' needs and abilities. Anticipating criticism of this model, Vygotsky (1986) would counter that while some dismiss "imitation [as] a mechanical activity that anyone can imitate . . . it is necessary to possess the means of stepping from something one knows to something new. With assistance, any child can do more than he can by himself—though only within the limits set by the state of his development" (187).

What does this process look like in a more advanced class? In short, it is much more efficient: I give my AP class the handout and ask them to develop one of each type of question about, for example, *Heart of Darkness* or *Their Eyes Are Watching God*. Whether they do this in class or for homework, the end is the same: To get them to take responsibility for their understanding and the subsequent discussion. I will usually have them get into groups to share their questions, telling them to first compare what they asked, then choose what they feel is the best question from their group. Once they have made that selection, I want them to be prepared to explain *why* that is the "best" question, then to use it to guide their own small-group discussion.

After they have had sufficient time to have a small-group discussion, during which time I am wandering around to evaluate their questions and the ensuing discussion, we convene as a full class and use their questions to guide a larger discussion. During such discussions the questions themselves are as much a part of the conversation as students' responses to them.

In some classes, especially those with more urgent instructional needs, I take a more intensive approach. Figure 2 shows an overhead from a program called *Academic Workout* (Burke 2007). While I follow pretty much the same steps just outlined when using this particular overhead, I ask students to work with it more closely, developing posters that describe the type of question and providing examples of that type of question in different subject areas (see Figure 3a and 3b). This deepens students' understanding of that question and their ability to generalize it into other areas.

Posters like these then remain on the wall for future and quick reference; they allow me to say, "take a minute and create a 'Think and Search' question about the chapter we have been discussing." The questions they develop then serve both to assess their understanding and to guide the discussion of the text,

82. Types of Questions

You may be asked four types of test questions. Each type requires its own special way to find the answer.

1. "Right There"	Sometimes these are called **factual questions.** These questions often use the same wording from the passage, which makes it easy to skim the text for the answer.
2. "Think and Search"	These are **interpretive questions.** Search, or **skim,** for ideas presented throughout the text and think about how they all go together.
3. "Author & You"	The answer to these questions is not in the text. You need to make an **inference** by adding what you learn from the author to what you already know.
4. "On My Own"	You can answer these questions without details from the text. The answer is based on your experiences.

Model

1. Right There What is the name of the team Greg wants to join?

2. Think and Search Why had Greg not been allowed to play for the high school team?

3. Author & You Why does Greg have a hard time in school?

4. On My Own Why do rewards motivate teens to work harder in school?

It wasn't often the Scorpions took on new players, especially 14-year-olds, and this was a chance of a lifetime for Greg. He hadn't been allowed to play high school ball, which he had really wanted to do, but playing for the community center team was the next best thing. Report cards were due in a week, and Greg had been hoping for the best.

Source: from "The Treasure of Lemon Brown" by Walter Dean Myers

Figure 2 The Types of Questions handout

From *Academic Workout: Reading and Language Arts,* 2007 (Curriculum Associates: North Billerica, MA).

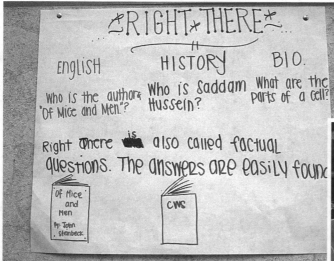

Figure 3a Detailed view of the "Right There" poster

Figure 3b Student drawing the "Right There" poster

ensuring that we are discussing aspects of it that interest students, while providing a more authentic context in which we can help them shape their own questions and raise them without dominating the discussion.

Other types of questions emerge naturally, usually appropriate to classes at all levels with some differentiation but often centered on issues of comprehension, importance, causes, effects, features, functions, and craft. In my AP Literature class, for example, we reached a point when reading *Crime and Punishment* where I felt we needed to pull back and look at the big picture—it was getting a bit fuzzy after four hundred pages. The goal was to determine the key events ("What happened?") and their importance ("Why is this important?/So what?").

To make it a bit more interesting and to get them to process the ideas on different levels, I created a timeline on the board (see Figure 4) and gave each student two sticky notes (one yellow, one blue). On the blue one, students wrote down the most crucial event that had *not* yet been identified on the board; on the yellow sticky note, they explained why this event was so important. Students arranged them on the board (see Figure 5) in chronological order, after which we used these to facilitate the discussion as a whole class.

Figure 4 A sticky note timeline: Notes on the top are blue; those on the bottom are yellow. Every student gets on of each color.

Figure 5 Toni posts her comments on the *Crime and Punishment* timeline.

Guiding Instruction Through Essential Questions

We are used to thinking of questions as things kids answer on tests or at the end of the chapter they read. Such test questions and study questions are not without value; however, questions can accomplish much more than merely checking what students learned or read. Throughout the book, my focus is on how to develop and use questions to:

- Prepare and help students participate in effective classroom discussion
- Connect what they learn to themselves, the world, and other texts or units they have studied
- Clarify and extend thinking about a subject
- Assess and deepen understanding of material
- Generate ideas and insights through reading, writing, representing, and discussing
- Organize instruction around big ideas and essential questions

It is this last idea—organizing instruction around big ideas and essential questions—that I want to explore in more detail because it is the central argument of this book. Structuring our "curriculum as [a] conversation" (Applebee 1996) will address three of the biggest challenges we face: engagement, comprehension, and retention. I do not mean to offer up this idea of curricular conversations as a silver bullet; as Applebee writes:

> It seems misguided to expect that an entire educational experience can be encompassed within one grand conversation—there are after all many different traditions of discourse that are valued in our culture, and a variety of intellectual tools that we hope students would master. On the other hand, there are real relationships among many of the separate conversations that now form the curriculum, and finding ways to examine their commonalities and differences can only be enriching. (83)

Wiggins and McTighe (2005) further validate the importance of big ideas in *Understanding by Design*, arguing that "big ideas . . . should be the focus of education for understanding. A big idea is a concept, theme, or issue that gives meaning and connection to discrete facts and skills" (5). Research on brain-based teaching (Jensen 2005; Willis 2006) consistently shows that such integrated, meaningful instruction is not only "enriching," but also highly effective in terms of engaging learners and teaching concepts.

The big question, of course, which Arthur Applebee and many others have tried to answer through their research, is *how* to create and sustain such conversations while at the same time teaching the skills and background knowledge needed to participate in them. In *Curriculum as Conversation*, Applebee goes on to say: "In helping students enter into curriculum domains, finding an initial topic or direction for conversation is critical. . . . It seems that most successful topics could be expressed as broad questions that invite discussion and debate across a broad domain of experiences" (1996, 83).

In her extensive research of middle and high school literacy instruction, Judith Langer (2002) found that "overt connections are constantly made between knowledge, skills, and ideas across lessons, classes, and grades" (23). Langer further emphasizes the importance of students connecting their learning in several distinct ways: "within lessons, across lessons, and across-in-school and out-of-school applications"; she concluded that "88 percent of effective teachers . . . make all three kinds of connections" (23).

Such connections, when based on questions students are "driven" to answer, play to the brain's strengths, allowing the students to "prime the pump" (Willis 2006) by asking "open-ended questions that do not have a single, definite, correct answer" (42), thereby becoming more "connected to their interests and experiences, [which keeps students] interested, especially if they receive encouragement for expressing their ideas" (42).

Alfred Tatum, in *Teaching Reading to Black Adolescent Males: Closing the Achievement Gap* (2005), reinforces the crucial role of such connections to students' interests and culture. Specifically, he suggests the following actions to engage and support African American boys (though I would add that *all* students benefit from these recommendations):

1. Engaging students with text and discussions about real issues they, their families, and their communities face, where students can analyze their lives in the context of the curriculum and discuss strategies for overcoming academic and societal barriers.

2. Using meaningful literacy activities that address students' cognitive and affective domains and that take into account the students' culture.

3. Connecting the social, the economic, and the political to the educational.

4. Acknowledging that developing skills, increasing test scores, and nurturing students' identity are fundamentally compatible.

5. Resolving the either-or dilemma of focusing on skill development or developing intelligence (54).

Tatum (2005) suggests such questions, and the freedom to ask them, determines the extent to which the student feels included in the class and curriculum. Echoing Neil Postman's remark that "all students [enter] school as questions," Tatum argues that *all* students come to school with questions they need to ask and discuss; however, if the teacher makes no room for such questions, students, especially African American boys, will feel shut out, unwelcome, and so turn away from the class—dismissing it as they feel it has dismissed them. Our students need us to listen to their questions. Their success, and ours, depend on it.

Let me end by returning to Gardner's "five minds for the future." Our students enter our schools and classrooms as apprentices once did a master's workshop or studio. Nystrand and others want us to cultivate in our students a "literate mind," which Judith Langer defined thus: "The kind of literate mind I care about involves the kind of thinking needed not only to do well in school, but outside of

school—in work and life. It is the kind of mind people need to do their jobs well, to adjust as their jobs change, and to be able change jobs when they need or want to" (2002). In this same address, Langer elaborated on her notion of being literate in the modern world:

> I see being literate as the ability to behave like a literate person—to engage in the kinds of thinking and reasoning people generally use when they read and write even in situations where reading and writing are not involved (such as the ability to inspect and analyze meanings from a variety of vantage points with or without texts—whether they have seen a movie or read a play, the mental act itself is a literate act). I call this ability "literate thinking."
>
> This view of literacy assumes individual and cultural differences and societal changes over time. It suggests that people use what they know and have experienced as a starting place for learning. It lets them start by manipulating their knowledge of content and their knowledge of language in ways that help them think and rethink their understandings. From this perspective, thinking and awareness are learned in the context of ideas and activities. My studies show that students who use literate thinking when no text is present can more easily learn to use it *with* text as well. This is a very different notion of literacy than thinking of literacy as the acquisition of a set of reading and writing skills and facts; and what one values as being smart and learning well, as well as how to teach and how you test it, are very different, as well.

Langer's observations about the literate mind recall Gardner's "five minds of the future"—the disciplinary, synthesizing, creating, respectful, and ethical minds he concludes are fundamental to the new world—but extend his notions of an educated mind which, he argues, is "likely to be crucial in a world marked by the hegemony of science and technology, global transmission of huge amounts of information, handling of routine tasks by computers and robots, and ever-increasing contacts of all sorts between diverse populations" (163).

In her final remarks about the literate mind, Langer says what I hope the rest of this book will help to enact: "I also want [students] to have choices—to be able to gain knowledge and learn new skills throughout their lives, to explore possibilities and ponder options as they shape and reshape their own lives and the world around them." That is what I want my class to accomplish, my students to leave knowing and having learned. Such a mind, prepared for whatever the future holds, is what the world expects, what the world needs—and what my students deserve.

An Intellectual Rite of Passage

Engaging Students with Essential Questions

The point is, to live everything. Live the questions now. Perhaps you will then gradually, without noticing it, live along some distant day into the answer.

—RAINER MARIA RILKE

Let us begin with the end: final exams and all that leads up to those last days in my freshman and senior English classes. After all, we often judge experiences based on how they end, not how they begin. Many counsel us, in both our personal and professional endeavors, to "to begin with the end in mind [which] means to start with a clear understanding of your destination. It means to know where you're going so that you better understand where you are now so that the steps you take are always in the right direction" (Covey 1989, 98).

Applying this notion of "backward design" to curriculum design, Wiggins and McTighe (2005) pose a series of design questions I hope the rest of this book will answer with useful examples from my own classroom:

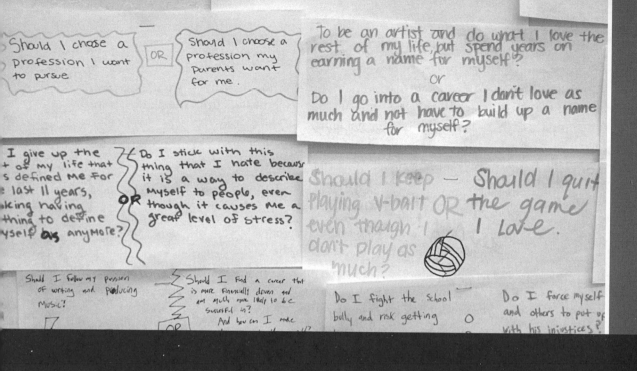

- What should students understand as a result of the activities or the content covered?

- What should the experiences or lectures equip students to do?

- How, then, should the activities or class discussions be shaped and processed to achieve the desired results?

- What would be evidence that learners are en route to the desired abilities and insights?

- How should all activities and resources be chosen and used to ensure that the learning goals are met and the most appropriate evidence produced?

- How will students be helped to see *by design* the purpose of the activity or resource and its helpfulness in meeting specific performance goals? (17)

Wiggins and McTighe summarize these questions and their backward design process in three stages: "(1) Identify the desired results; (2) Determine acceptable evidence; and (3) Plan learning experiences and instruction" (18).

Perhaps my favorite and most useful question of all is, "What is the problem for which *x* is the solution?" This is a question that clarifies even as it challenges, helping me cut through the rationalizations that come so easily to so many of us

as we are planning our classes, envisioning our semesters from the relative tranquility of those last weeks of summer and/or winter break.

For me, as for most of you reading this book, I face *several* problems for which the spring semester final exam is the solution:

- Students grow increasingly disengaged, especially seniors, as the year comes to an end.

- Students have knowledge and skills, mandated by state standards, that they must learn and demonstrate to their teachers.

- Students have all sorts of skills and interests that school often does not give them occasion to use or pursue, thus rendering the curriculum too often impersonal and, in the eyes of many students, irrelevant.

- Students face increasingly complex personal and professional demands that we must play our part in preparing them to meet, especially as they relate to working, thinking, and communicating.

- Students need assignments and assessments that develop and measure enduring understandings not surface skills or facts they will forget by the time they finish taking the final exam.

Of course, these concerns are not, by any means, limited to the end of the year; while these challenges grow in April and May, they are with us from the moment the kids enter the class in the fall.

These expectations are all well and good, but *what does it look like* to "teach with questions"? To answer that you will have to come into my senior English class in the final weeks of the year. While it would be somewhat logical to begin with my freshman class, I think it's best to go right to the most dangerous place on the map: second semester seniors. A little background is useful: These are Advanced Placement (AP) English Literature classes of thirty-three students, all of whom plan to attend colleges (from junior college to Harvard), have completed the AP exams, and now have only two weeks until they graduate. We've worked hard all year to improve their analytical reading and writing, during which time they have communicated their insights through multiple means and media, as well as in small-group and full-class discussions.

But it's late May on the California coast, the sun is out, and their attention is often as minimal as their clothing. But *I* don't have senioritis, and I want my days spent doing meaningful, engaging work that still has one last chance (do we *ever* give up?) of making that difference; of doing that assignment that years later students will say, "You know, right at the end of my senior year I had to do this as-

signment and it got me thinking and ended up being the most important thing I did in high school. . . . "

Despite all these challenges, the finals begin, spread out over a week, and great things happen (most of the time). Despite Postman's dour assessment that students "enter as question marks and graduate as periods," my seniors are concluding semester-long investigations guided by big questions such as:

- How do you measure and maximize human worth?

- How does war affect those who experience it and their families?

- What does the future look like?

- What most influences the choices we make?

- How does the environment in which we live or are raised shape us?

- How and why does our relationship with our parents change as we grow up?

It is this last question that was posed by Claire, whose grades in the home stretch embody the increasingly disaffected seniors (who are "*so* out of here" as they would say). We will examine the question in detail, but it will be useful to know what the actual assignment was before we see what Claire and the others did for this final assignment. Figure 1.1 shows the handout I gave the students in January.

Here is a sample proposal submitted by one of my students:

A full-size version of this handout, customizable and reproducible, is available at www. heinemann.com.

AP Inquiry Project:
Independent Reading Requirement Proposal

Danielle Bakhtiari

Subject of Inquiry: Murder and dehumanization of innocent people from different places in the world. (Cambodia, Sudan, and Dominican Republic)

Guiding Question: What enables humans to survive the horrors found in other parts of the world? How and why are people from these different places mistreated and stripped of their humanity?

Rationale: Personally, I was looking for stories that are appealing and interesting. We do not always hear about these faraway places that have corrupt governments, no money, and people struggling to survive day by day. These three books will give me an insight about a world of different innocent people struggling to survive the harsh realities. This will also teach me to learn about and be thankful for where I live and remember there are places where things are bad and the people need help.

AP Inquiry Project: Independent Reading Requirement and Spring Final

Overview: Each of you has subjects of particular interest to you that school rarely gives you the opportunity to investigate. This assignment outlines the second-semester reading requirement. The purpose of this semester's independent reading assignment remains the same as it was last semester: to prepare you for the AP exam on May 8. In addition, however, I want each of you to leave your senior year having investigated a topic of great personal interest in depth, by using several different books you choose.

Requirements

Each student must:

- Read *three* books by semester's end, all of them AP-level novels (though you can, if you wish, substitute one novel with a relevant nonfiction book).
- Read one book per grading period.
- Write in-class essays on the first two books as we have done all year; these essays will be based on your own BQs (Big Questions).
- Submit a written proposal that includes everything outlined below.
- Investigate your subject through at least three other sources, all of which must be included in your bibliography.
- Perform, produce, or present your final project; it must incorporate all *three* books (during the last week of the semester and on the day of the final).
- Turn in a typed annotated bibliography of independent books that includes:
  - Introduction that clearly identifies the Big Question you sought to answer this semester, *briefly* explains *why* this subject interests you, and identifies (in *bullets*) the three main conclusions you drew from your study of this topic through these books.
  - Title, author, publisher, publication date, city, and number of pages (i.e., complete and proper citation information for each book).
  - Approximately seventy-five (75) words that explain not only what the book was about but also how it related to your Big Question.

Proposal

Each student must submit a typed, one-page proposal (see example on the back) by next Monday; it should include the following:

- *The subject of your inquiry* (nature, science, relationships, Africa, self-image)
- *A guiding question* (or questions) about this subject (e.g., What is mankind's place in the natural world?)
- *A rationale* for why you want to study this subject all semester
- *A summary* of what you know about this subject at this time
- *A prediction* about what you think you will discover during your investigation
- *The titles and authors* of the three books you will read this semester
- *A discussion* as to the importance of this subject (which answers the questions, "So what?")
- *Other possible sources* (websites, publications, people, organizations) you might consult to satisfy the three "additional sources."

Sample Set

Here is a sample set of three books you might read as part of this investigation:

- *The Places in Between*, Rory Stewart
- *What Is the What?* Dave Eggers
- *The Sheltering Sky,* Paul Bowles
  Each of these books charts the experiences of people in foreign countries who are on journeys to escape from or discover something. All are set in Muslim countries, one of them describing Rory Stewart's walking trip through Afghanistan after the fall of the Taliban.

Note: Students must read the books listed on their proposal; you may, if you learn of new and more relevant titles, revise but *please check with me first.*

Figure 1.1

Summary: At this time, I do not know a whole lot about what I am deciding to read. That is what I think is going to make my whole experience better and more intriguing. I will be able to read these stories and learn about so much from different places of the world, and therefore become a more knowledgeable person about these different places.

Prediction: Reading these three stories will open my eyes to how bad different places can really be. I will see how horrible humans can be to other humans and learn to be more grateful of the place that I live. I also know that these stories will make me sad and wish I could do something to save innocent people's humanity.

Titles and Authors:

1) *They Poured Fire on Us from the Sky*, Alphonsion Deng
2) *To Destroy You Is No Loss*, Joan D. Criddle
3) *In the Time of the Butterflies*, Julia Alvarez

Importance: It is important for people to be aware of what is going on in different parts of the world, especially when innocent people are being murdered and dehumanized. It helps us become familiar with a world and other cultures that we do not know. Such knowledge will help us in the future by allowing us to learn from previous horrific mistakes. Also, people need to understand that not all places are as peaceful and wonderful as the United States of America.

Other Possible Sources: To further aid my study of this topic, I can listen to world news reports, look for newspaper articles, talk to people who help places with genocide and evil dictatorships, and look up websites about the genocides and different dictatorships and the effects of the innocent human beings.

Students had the semester to complete the assignment, reading one book every six weeks in addition to the required texts we were reading and essays they were writing. At the end of the first two grading periods (every six weeks), students write an in-class essay on the book they read for their project, basing the essay on how the book relates to their final topic. They use the Thesis Generator (Figure 1.2) and their original guiding question for their project to develop their own topic. An example of one such in-class essay follows; this one was written by Chris Schmidt as an investigation of war and its effects on those who fight. Figure 1.3 shows the AP Essay Scoring Rubric that was used for the same project.

A full-size version of each of these handouts, customizable and reproducible, is available at www.heinemann.com.

Thesis Generator

Topic: Compare and contrast the different types of relationships humans have with nature. Include examples from your own experience and the different texts we have read or viewed. After comparing and contrasting, make a claim about what you feel are our rights and responsibilities toward the natural world in general. Provide reasons and evidence to support your claim.

Example

1. Identify the *subject* of your paper.	Relationships between teenagers and their parents
2. Turn your subject into a guiding question.	How does the relationship between teenagers and their parents change?
3. Answer your question with a statement.	As teens grow more independent, they resent and resist the limitations and expectations their parents impose on them.
4. Refine this statement into a *working* thesis.	Conflict between teenagers and their parents is a difficult but necessary stage in kids' development.

1. Identify the *subject* of your paper.	
2. Turn your subject into a guiding question.	
3. Answer your question with a statement.	
4. Refine this statement into a *working* thesis.	

Figure 1.2

AP Essay Scoring Rubric

Student: _____

Paper: _____ Score: _____

Score	Description
9–8 **A+/A**	❏ responds to the prompt clearly, directly, and fully ❏ approaches the text analytically ❏ supports a coherent thesis with evidence from the text ❏ explains how the evidence illustrates and reinforces its thesis ❏ employs subtlety in its use of the text and the writer's style is fluent and flexible ❏ has no mechanical and grammatical errors
7–6 **A–/B+**	❏ responds to the assignment clearly and directly but with less development than an 8–9 paper ❏ demonstrates a good understanding of the text ❏ supports its thesis with appropriate textual evidence ❏ analyzes key ideas but lacks the precision of an 8–9 essay ❏ uses the text to illustrate and support in ways that are competent but not subtle ❏ written in a way that is forceful and clear with few grammatical and mechanical errors
5 **B**	❏ addresses the assigned topic intelligently but does not answer it fully and specifically ❏ shows a good but general grasp of the text ❏ uses the text to frame an apt response to the prompt ❏ employs textual evidence sparingly or offers evidence without attaching it to the thesis ❏ written in a way that is clear and organized but may be somewhat mechanical ❏ marred by conspicuous grammatical and mechanical errors
4–3 **B–/C**	❏ fails in some important way to fulfill the demands of the prompt ❏ does not address part of the assignment ❏ provides no real textual support for its thesis ❏ bases its analysis on a misreading of some part of the text ❏ presents one or more incisive insights among others of less value ❏ written in a way that is uneven in development with lapses in organization and clarity ❏ undermined by serious and prevalent errors in grammar and mechanics

2–1
 	
D/F
	❏ combines two or more serious failures:
	  ❏ does not address the actual assignment
	  ❏ indicates a serious misreading of the text (or suggest the student did *not* read it)
	  ❏ does not offer textual evidence
	  ❏ uses textual evidence in a way that suggests a failure to understand the text
	  ❏ is unclear, badly written, or unacceptably brief
	  ❏ is marked by egregious errors
	  ❏ is written with great style but devoid of content (rare but possible)

Comments

_____

_____

_____

_____

_____

Figure 1.3

The most primal need of humans is our desire to have companionship. In *Tree of Smoke*, Denis Johnson intertwines the need for companionship with survival. As the various characters progress in their journeys, they are constantly working to make connections with others. But when war becomes involved in those relationships, complications arise. The absence of human contact, or the loss of it, has serious mental implications. The Vietnam War produced previously unheard of numbers of veterans who returned home with mental illnesses. Because of this new type of war, where casualties skyrocketed, and support on the home-front disintegrated, countless men were returned to their families less than whole.

Early on in the novel, the relationship between Skip Bonds and Kathy Jones is a perfect example of a person's need to connect with another. Skip is a man following orders from unknown men in a land that he is trying to escape. After the news of her husband's death, Kathy is lost, without foundation, somewhere in the Philippines. Both of these foreigners are disillusioned by the Philippine culture which represents a vast difference from the western culture they were raised in. In each other they find that something that is familiar, that they can rely on for support.

On the other hand, James Houston, a high school student in Arizona, is being held down by meaningless relationships that are hurting his development as a man. He pities his mother in her struggle to make a living working on a ranch, and he is unable to find substance in his relationships with his peers. His time with Stevie is simply his way of fulfilling his primitive instinct to "get laid." Once she lets him go all the way, and his goal is achieved, he realizes that he still needs a deeper connection. So he flees the environment where he has no room to grow and he enlists in the Army. Even as he is finishing his basic training, James starts to fear the death that awaits him in Vietnam.

As Skip continues his journey to find something fulfilling, he is presented with an unusual circumstance around the death of Father Carrigan. He feels that he is being led in circles, sent by his uncle to learn of this man, he feels deceived when his uncle's henchmen arrive to kill the man he was sent to see.

As the story progresses toward the war in Vietnam, the characters' relationships become tense and begin to deteriorate away from them. They are being thrown toward a probable death by their own country, and worst of all, their own families are protesting against the work they are trying to do. Lost in a world where simple actions must be judged on

their personal, skewed conscience, the men become overwhelmed by their surroundings.

Because of the absence of connections to people they need to rely on, and surrounded by the deaths of their compatriots, friends, and allies, their minds become warped by all of the various problems they are faced with. As a result of these issues, the men are mentally unstable and become [some] of the many veterans who returned from this new war, less than men.

Extensions of Inquiry

The semester final, however, can't be an essay as I have no way to grade all those papers the week they graduate (especially since our grades for seniors are due a week before graduation). Besides, getting them to write essays would make Sisyphus' task look like a stroll through the garden. In addition to the work required (as outlined previously), I asked each student to turn in material on the day of the final, based on the handout shown in Figure 1.4, and give a *brief* presentation.

A full-size version of this handout, customizable and reproducible, is available at www. heinemann.com.

The night before her final, Claire sent an urgent email asking for last-minute help. Does it bother me that she "wants a good grade"? Not at all, because I am just thrilled to see a senior engaged and committed, working hard to meet my (and her own) high standards. Here is her email:

Hello Mr. Burke,

So I'm putting together my final for tomorrow, and I'm having trouble figuring out the best way to articulate what I want to say.

What I ended up doing was collecting personal note cards from people I knew, neighbors, strangers and such about their relationships with children or parents then putting them into a notebook (PostSecret.com inspired, many are anonymous, some are signed). I'm attempting to get these on to a PowerPoint, but I'm not sure how that will fare just yet.

Many are very interesting to say the least and I love what I have gotten done so far . . . just not sure where I should go from here. Ultimately, I want a good grade to be honest.

Claire Hickey

AP Follow-up to Inquiry: Final Exam

Overview
This semester you have read three books, each one exploring a theme or subject common to the others. The premise was to examine a subject from different perspectives. Now it's time to wrap it all up and think about what you read, then share that learning with the rest of us in a way we will find interesting and you will find challenging.

Invitation
This may well be the last piece of thinking you do in high school, so I want something not just good, or even great, but something intriguing and remarkable. So, the first step is to find a way to connect all three books that draws on your individual intellectual strengths—your creative talents. Thus, you must find some idea common to all three books aside from, for example, that they all have to do with love of or living in a foreign country. Then represent that idea in one of the following ways (or some other way you come up with):

- Metaphor
- Symbol
- Equation
- Thought problem
- Diagram (or other visual explanation)
- Poem
- Artwork (or other visual representation, including photograph)
- Video (must be short!)
- Musical interpretation
- Dramatic interpretation
- Surprise me!

This first part is not meant to be some massive project in itself, though it is meant to challenge you to show us both what you can do at your best in your area of greatest talent.

You must also write a paragraph that explains the meaning and purpose behind your product in this first step. If, for example, you created a visual metaphor (e.g., a drawing of a seed that opens up into a blossom to visually represent the effect of love on people), you would then write a paragraph explaining your idea and the visual metaphor.

Paper
In addition to the opportunity just outlined, you will write a *one-page typed paper* that discusses the three books you read and what you learned from them about the subject you explored. **List the three books and their authors at the top of your paper, please.** Guiding questions might include:

- What was my subject and why did I want to explore it?
- What did these authors say about this subject?
- What interesting similarities and differences did I notice?
- How do these authors' ideas about this subject compare with my own?
- What did I realize, or learn, that surprised me most about this subject after exploring it for a semester?

Figure 1.4

Here is what Claire turned in the day of her final:

Claire Hickey
May 19, 2008
English Burke AP, Second Semester

Inquiry Project Topic: Parent-Child Relationships

I chose this topic because it is one which affects us all, as mothers, fathers, daughters, sons, grandparents or grandchildren. My own relationship with my parents over the past few years, and the effect the loss of my uncle has had on my grandparents, were all reasons I chose this topic. The note cards were a great addition to the topic, due to the fact that it allowed an even larger number of responses, rather than just relying on the literature and my own personal experiences.

The conclusions I found are difficult to articulate, and more of an understanding than anything else:

- The degree to which we care for another, and are willing to put our own selves out for another, particularly our own children, illustrates an interesting complex of the human condition. While we typically display an almost savage, natural side, as can be seen in McCarthy's *The Road* and books such as Golding's *Lord of the Flies*, the way we treat our offspring shows off a totally different side of ourselves.

- Father and mother figures are imperative in a child's life, whether in forming a child's morals, guiding them or simply being a physical comfort. However, these figures aren't necessarily biological, and occasionally biological parents can be harmful to a child.

- Parent-child relationships are complex in the nature that every choice, every decision and every conversation can turn the relationship, and have both positive and negative effects. Timing is also key, and learning to accept your son/daughter/mother/father for who they are, and not who you believe they are supposed to be.

- As parents and children, we will never completely understand each other, and if we can accept that, we will build a strong bond.

Coetzee, J. M. *Disgrace*. New York: Penguin. 2000. (220 pages)

> *Disgrace* took me to another degree of a father and daughter relationship, focusing on a father who ultimately ruins his career when he has an affair with a young student in his class. Moving in with his daughter on her farm in South Africa, he attempts to change her, or even in a

sense, mold her, to be what he believes she should be. She sticks to her own ideals and in turn this confuses him. After an incident in which they were both attacked and Lucy raped, he struggles with his position as her father, struggling to define what the word "father" itself should mean. In the end, the experience betters David, who finally learns that his daughter is an individual and has chosen the right path, while he realizes he may not have.

Hosseini, Khaled. *The Kite Runner*. New York: Riverhead Books, 2003. (371 pages)

A novel which everyone apparently read except me until now, I found it interesting to say the least. A great story, one that truly stands out. I attempted to focus on Sohrab's relationship with Amir in the United States, his own loss of a mother and father and ultimately Amir's desire to please his father, Baba, as a child. Overall, this novel shows the core of human nature and the necessity we feel to care for and be cared for by another. The influence our parents have on us as children and we have on them as parents is quite grand, and as cliché as it sounds, we never realize how important it is until it's gone.

Kidd, Sue Monk. *The Secret Life of Bees*. New York: Penguin Books. 2003. (302 pages)

This novel not only explores the relationship between Lily Owens and how she deals with her mother's death, but also the relationship between Lily and her African American "mothers." I found this book fascinating because it presented a unique situation which was a strong addition to my study of this subject. Her relationship with her father, and his eventual realization that it would be best to let her go in the end, was another component which I enjoyed. Most important was the idea that mothers and fathers aren't always biological, and those which are biological might not be the best figures in our lives.

McCarthy, Cormac. *The Road*. Toronto: Random House. 2006. (287 pages)

At the end the end of the world, or so it seems, a father and son attempt to survive among dust and a barren landscape full of cannibals. The horror that they face every day, the extremities they go to, are unbelievable. The father's perseverance to get his son to safety, despite his own inevitable death, truly show the effort a parent will go to in order to give their child a better life. Interesting ideas came up throughout the story, such as possibly having to kill his son, and the way cannibals treated each other.

Figure 1.5 Claire presents her senior project on family relationships to the class at the end of the year.

Figure 1.6 Samples of Claire's project

I never thought I would be the son who loses touch with their parents after they graduate from college and get a job and girl friend and become adult. But I haven't been home since February and they only live in San Diego.

I thought my mom was superwoman when I was a kid. She's a lot more human now.

— Jeff

The one reason I wanted children is so I would have people around me that would laugh at all my stupid jokes and fall for all my magic tricks and would in turn make me laugh all day long. It worked for a while.

During the week my dad works down in San Diego so my mom is home alone most of the time and she is always running around for my sister and me. I really appreciate how much she does for us. she ♥ is AMAZING

My parents have always been tough on me because I am the oldest child I hated all the crap they put me through and hate even more watching my brother and sister get off everything easy. I guess the hardest thing about parenting is letting your kids grow up and admitting to yourself you can't hold on.

I think the hardest thing about my childhood was that it seemed my parents saw in me who they wanted me to be rather than who I was. As a mother, I have always tried to love and affirm my daughter for who she is now, not if she changed into how I need her. Perfect just how she is. That's how children should feel.

My memory of my mother runs the gauntlet from our time as children. She was very religious. We said rosary every night. Whenever things were tough, she found strength in her unbelievable faith. While I recall some real happy times — weddings, birth of my first child — nothing will ever rival the day that she died for sadness.

I used to hate my father. He controlled everything. He has OCPD (basically meaning nothing is ever good enough). I would always paint with my grandpa to get away. It was an escape, freedom. Now I realize I need both my tyrant of a father and hippie of a grandpa to be me, balanced and complete. Now, I can thank them.

I LOVE MY PARENTS MORE THAN ANYTHING IN THE WORLD THEY PUSH ME TO DO MY BEST CONSTANTLY

I LOVE THEM!

I know nothing about my father :) ...but I love him

It took a long time—well into middle age—for me to realize that my parents weren't the ideal parents that I had internalized them as being. They were imperfect, their parenting was flawed, and they passed detrimental as well as positive attributes to their children. It was difficult for me to admit this, because I felt that to do so would represent a betrayal, a disloyalty to them. I now realize that this isn't so. My parents raised me as best they could, and just because I see where they fell short, it in no way discounts their love and effort.

Figure 1.6 Samples of Claire's project (*continued*)

Claire offers an engaging yet somewhat traditional print-based final project, but most worked to produce more media-based final productions, reinforcing the extent to which many of today's graduates are fluent in and engaged by literacies we are still struggling to incorporate into our curriculum. As I mentioned earlier, Chris Schmidt investigated war and its effects on soldiers, and collaborated with several other boys who explored related questions, such as the "darkness in the human heart," and whether there is such a thing as a just war. They decided to work together because they shared not only a common subject but also a mutual interest in filmmaking. Ultimately, the boys collaborated to create an engaging fifteen-minute original film for which they also wrote the script.

As with Claire, they had to do more than just press the Play button and stand back. They had to situate their film in the context of their inquiries, explaining how it related to the questions they were trying to answer. Their film was a serious effort, an engaging stop-action movie that involved multiple cameras, careful editing in iMovie, and a dynamic soundtrack filled with well-chosen songs from the Vietnam era.

Here is Chris Schmidt's write-up, which they all had to turn in the day of the final:

Christopher Schmidt
English Lit & Comp

The Consequences of War

Mankind has always engaged in war; it has become an accepted part of life. Perhaps in the past it was simply ignored, but as mode[rn] warfare has evolved, a new form of casualty has emerged. Countless numbers of soldiers have returned from recent wars with more than mere physical wounds; they have returned psychologically damaged. This side-effect of war is something that the military has attempted to ignore. After Vietnam, the U.S. Department of Veteran Affairs refused to acknowledge the mental problems of many Americans returning from overseas, and as a result they were refused much-needed medical care. Through the reading of the following books, I intended to research the source of these mental problems and how they were dealt with in postwar environments.

Figure 1.7 Raymond, Owen, and Chris presenting

Conclusions

- A major element in the development of these mental illnesses is the loss of human contact. It is clear early on in *Tree of Smoke* that individuals do not function well in the absence of human interaction.

- The debate and anger that was building up in the homeland created a hostile and charged environment for the veterans to return to. A major reason why the Veterans Administration was so adamant about denying mental issues was because they had become so defensive as a result of a hostile counterculture.

- The mental issues of war are by no means new. As shown in *For Whom the Bell Tolls*, a story about early 20th-century warfare, few can survive war without suffering some physical or mental harm. A major reason why these issues became so prominent after Vietnam is that by that time we actually had treatments for these problems.

Johnson, Denis. *Tree of Smoke*. New York: Farrar, Straus and Giroux. 2007. 614.

> This novel portrays several characters in their journey to and through Vietnam. As a whole, the characters feel a constant need to find companionship in such an isolating setting. With few others to connect to, the characters start losing touch with reality. James Houston becomes distraught with his situation in America; he feels out of touch with the people he knows, and turns to the army for escape. Unfortunately, as he completes training, he realizes that the army is not the best escape option as it is leading him to an almost certain death. The suffering portrayed by the characters in this novel results in the mental illnesses that have become the center of my research.

Hemingway, Ernest. *For Whom the Bell Tolls*. New York: Scribner. 1940. 471.

> Hemingway offers a detailed description of a young man brought to fight in the Spanish Civil War in the early 20th century. Robert Jordan, the main character, is an American brought in to aid a side that he is told to fight for. As he progresses into the war, he realizes that he is not killing big bad Fascists, but is, in fact, killing men who have been brought on in the name of Fascism to fight for this idea they do not even understand. He becomes challenged by this idea and begins to lose his sense of control. This simple moment of understanding disables him and begins to cause him great mental anguish. This occurrence is an example of mental suffering experienced in an older form of warfare. While the more recognized forms of mental health resulting from war came out of Vietnam, there were certainly issues occurring in war well before that.

Maraniss, David. *They Marched Into Sunlight*. New York: Simon & Schuster. 2003. 592.

> This nonfiction book revolves around two settings, one being a battle in Vietnam, the other a protest in Madison, Wisconsin. The two settings illustrate the contrast between a soldier's point of view, and the point of view of someone on the home front. This book describes the environment that eventually became a burden for soldiers returning home from Vietnam. While the protesters were a necessary part in ending the war, their actions created a hostile environment that was far from beneficial for soldiers returning psychologically unstable.

This semester-long investigation of these subjects amounts to a personal quest, an intellectual rite of passage for these students. It is time for them to take

the reins of their own education for the moment, showing themselves and me not only what they have learned but also that they want to learn, that they have subjects they are hungry to know more about as they prepare to leave my class and our high school for the larger arena of work and college. All the work Chris, or Claire, or any of the others did over the semester is its own reward; and as they arrive at the final, they are clearly eager to share it, to challenge themselves one last time on the final before packing up and graduating.

They do not arrive at this final day unprepared, nor having been left to their own devices. Seniors are already rudderless enough! Moreover, students who are guided by questions need help learning how to steer their way through such uncharted waters. Without guidance and accountability, students can wander from the topic they are investigating, arriving at the final with little more than a summary or an extended digression. To keep my seniors on course, I meet with them regularly in the weeks prior to the days of final presentations, taking advantage of the many interruptions (Senior Day, AP exams, graduation orientations—common during this time of the senior year) to arrange such individual conferences. I don't need to meet with each student long, some not at all if they show clear evidence of being on track. Usually I sit on the side with individual students to pose a few routine questions about problems they are encountering, resources that might help, solutions they could consider, what percentage of their project is done, and how they plan to present it to the class. (See Figure 1.8.)

Prior to these meetings, I ask students to write down the question they are investigating on an index card, what they plan to do for their final, how long they

Figure 1.8 My conference with senior Hannah Pham

would like in class, and what their needs will be when they present. I need to know the length of the presentation so that I can schedule the five days we will take for all the finals, the fifth day being the two-hour final period itself.

While it is important to get the logistics worked out during these conferences, it is much more important that we discuss their actual final production because it should reflect a deep understanding of their subject and what they are able to do when it comes to communicating by one means or another, one medium or another. Thus, my primary role at this point is to pose questions, such as the following, while consulting the index card they filled out:

- What is your subject?
- What is the question you were trying to answer about that subject?
- What is the point you want to convey to us about this subject?
- What are some of the key ideas that emerged from your investigation of this question?
- How will you convey these insights and ideas you learned while investigating this question?
- Why is that (e.g., a video, painting, series of poems, monologue) the best way to convey the insights into your subject?
- What you are saying is good, but it sounds like you might end up with a visual summary of the books if you do that. How will you avoid such a limited response to the big question you are asking?

As the finals begin, it is evident that this careful planning and guidance paid off, since students offer, from the very first one, remarkable presentations that give us all plenty to think about. Each one is different, but all share the same quality.

As Brittany Martinez steps up to begin the finals in the first period, she brings with her adult twins, two men with whom her father works, both of whom were adopted and raised by different families. Thus begins her presentation, part of which includes a discussion with the twins about how our environment and experiences shape us. Throughout her twenty-minute presentation, which everyone is clearly interested in, she poses excellent questions to the twins, and connects their comments and her own findings to the literature she read during the semester.

Once the applause dies down, Matt G. gets up and writes a big mathematical equation he created on the board then turns and asks, "How can we measure and

Figure 1.9 Hanayo read three apocalyptic novels—*The Road*, *Oryx and Crake*, and *The Pesthouse*—that she represented in her original painting; it shows a source of light streaming down on a lone person in the midst of all the ruins.

Figure 1.10 Trevor and his multimedia Africa presentation

maximize human potential?" And so our finals go. (Figures 1.9 and 1.10 show two other students making their presentations.) All of the seniors have asked questions they want to understand but realize they will need their whole lives to answer.

BACK TO THE BEGINNING: SUMMER READING AND THE START OF THE SCHOOLYEAR

Before students even enter my senior class in August, they know they'll be required to think, to ask questions, to make connections. This unit began with the end of the year. It only makes sense, then, to end with how the year began: their summer reading requirement prior to beginning the year with me. Instead of just choosing a couple classics or contemporary AP-level books and telling students to read and take notes on them, I want my students to have a conversation with themselves and the books about a subject that matters to them. I know that most of my kids will not study literature in college; yet they have emerging and serious interests, areas of strength such as science, psychology, economics, politics, and war (given the era in which they live). Thus my summer reading assignment, shown in Figure 1.11, offers them pairs of books they can choose, depending on their area of interest.

A full-size version of this handout, customizable and reproducible, is available at www. heinemann.com.

AP Literature Summer Reading

Mr. Burke

Overview

Incoming AP Literature students are required to read several books over the summer in preparation for the course and subsequent AP exam. One portion of the AP exam, the Free Response essay, demands that students have a wide range of challenging literary works on which they can draw when writing that essay. The goal of this summer's reading, however, is not to prepare you for the exam but to initiate you into the conversation about ideas through books by both contemporary and classic authors.

AP Literature *is* college; it not a preparation for college. If you are looking for ways around this reading assignment, you should not enroll in this class.

Students who do not complete the summer reading—all of it, as spelled out by these guidelines—will not be eligible to take the course.

If you have any questions, write to me at jburke@englishcompanion.com.

Requirements

Each student must do the following:

- Choose one pair of books from the following list of books.

- Read the chosen books, taking notes or annotating as needed to help you do well on the in-class essay on these books. These notes are for you: I will not collect or evaluate them.

- Purchase, read, and annotate *How to Read Literature Like a Professor* by Thomas C. Foster. (Note: There are *many* used copies of this book on Amazon.com for only a couple dollars.)

- Write an in-class essay on the books in which you use the ideas from Foster's book as a guide to analyze the literature you read.

Titles

The following pairs of books comprise a conversation that should take place between you, the authors, and their characters. The books share a common idea that should be clear enough by the time you finish reading them. While there is no required order, you might consider reading Foster's book first as a way of preparing to read the two novels.

1. *Beowulf* (Seamus Heaney translation)
   Going After Cacciato, Tim O'Brien

2. *Caramelo*, Sandra Cisneros
   The Waves, Virginia Woolf

3. *The Book Thief* (by Marcus Zusak)
   Obasan, Joy Kagawa

4. *The Reluctant Fundamentalist*, Mohsin Hamid
   The Fall, Albert Camus

Figure 1.11

When it comes to developing independence and a love of reading, we want to provide as many opportunities as possible to help students, even AP Lit seniors, to get into "the reading zone," which Nancie Atwell (2007) describes as "more of a zone than a state . . . a place where readers went when they left our classroom behind and lived vicariously in their books" (21). Even more than the "zone," I want students, these rambunctious seniors about to graduate, to enter into other selves, other realities, trying them on en route to the person they will eventually become.

So begins a year we spend asking and investigating questions that help students with those bigger, more personal questions about who they are, what they should be, why they are here. We spend the year with Antigone and Hamlet, Raskolnikov and Marlow, Sophocles and Conrad, Faulkner and Hesse, who, like Hamlet himself, wonders what he should be, how he should live. As the questions in Figure 1.12 suggest, when given the opportunity to ask themselves, "To be _____ or not to be _____?", our students have a lot to say, so much they want to ask, and even more they still want to know.

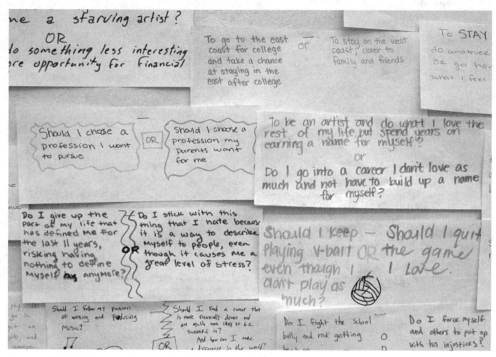

Figure 1.12 Hamlet questions on the classroom wall

Spirited Inquiry

Creating Questions to Access a Challenging Text

"There was a time when people used literature to think."
—PHILIP ROTH, FROM *EXIT GHOST*

In advanced classes, teachers should be asking demanding, sophisticated questions that challenge students' assumptions and force them to engage in divergent thinking; more importantly, however, the students themselves should be learning which questions to ask, when to ask them, and how to investigate and formulate an intelligent response to them. We need generative, analytical, creative thinkers—the ones who will bring imagination to their work. We do not need students who are obedient—those who think as they are directed; that way of thinking will ensure our country's decline and its intellectual ruin. To prevent such a fate, we must foster a culture of innovation within our classrooms—one defined by a spirit of inquiry into big ideas. In their English framework, the Partnership for 21st Century Skill and National Council of Teachers of English (2008) emphasize similar intellectual "outcomes" that echo the habits of mind we dis-

WHO SACRIFICES	WHAT	WHY _FOR WHAT REASON_	SO WHAT? _WHY IS IT IMPORTANT?_
onya	· her self · her body · her youth · her dignity	· to support family · to protect children	Reveals her character. that she is accepts res for others.

cussed earlier; they balance creativity and innovation as well as critical thinking and problem solving. These principles are especially relevant to the discussion at hand.

Sternberg and Grigorenko (2007) synthesize these cognitive strands into a "triarchic" view of intelligence that combines analytical, creative, and practical abilities to account for what they call "successful intelligence" (10). But what does this all look like in the classroom, especially in an AP class full of anxiety-ridden seniors whose minds are consumed by college acceptance worries? I accept that my AP seniors enter class intent on studying, it sometimes seems, everything *but* English when they go to college. Although my class is always about the ideas literature asks us to consider, the questions it demands that we ask, it is also about the world the students must enter and the skills they need if they are to thrive there. So without attempting to turn literature into a case study of poor business decisions, or the habits of highly effective people, I design an experience that attempts to cultivate in my students innovation, collaboration, and disciplined intelligence, through the study of literature and those questions it raises.

Crime and Punishment: The Big Idea

While I use questions throughout the year in my classes, I want students to take more responsibility for developing and using the questions in the second semester when we read what is the most challenging book of the year: *Crime and Punishment.* In this class, with thirty-five seniors who are increasingly restless, I need to provide a more responsive curriculum that allows them to take the wheel. The following assignment can be adapted to any grade level, really, but in this case we are talking about my AP Literature class, a class made up of kids who already know what they want to study in college and so have declared interests. Instead of ignoring these interests, I want to tap into them. The following assignment allows me to do that in different ways while still playing a key instructional role throughout the six-week unit.

Before my students read the first page of the book, I give them the following "Investigation" handout and ask them to decide which topic interests them the most. This, I tell them, is the "lens" through which they will read the whole book, taking notes on and paying attention to those details related to, for example, "faith." Students now have a personal purpose, one connected to a subject that intrigues them, that they can use to guide their reading. Such a purpose makes them more active, intentional readers who have a mental compass by which they can steer themselves through the vast waters of a demanding text. What's more, the notes they take will prepare them for not only the subsequent presentations and their culminating paper, but also the daily discussions and weekly blog conversations that are required. Figure 2.1 shows the assignment, accompanied by the handy checklist (Figure 2.2), which is provided to keep students organized and make my expectations clear.

A full-size version of each of these handouts, customizable and reproducible, is available at www. heinemann.com.

Extending Inquiry Online

Guided by their chosen topic and the questions they have generated about it, students begin reading Dostoevsky, taking notes and annotating as they see fit. They soon begin discussing the topics, posing and responding to their own and others' questions in several different contexts. Every week each student must participate in the online discussion about that topic, reading and responding to others' postings, as Figure 2.3 shows. At my school, we use a program called School Loop (www.schoolloop.com; I've directed students to this resource in the

INVESTIGATION: *Crime and Punishment*

Burke / AP English

Overview

Every book explores different subjects. It is our interest in these subjects and our desire to answer them that guides our own reading. This assignment asks you to choose from a list of topics, each of which Fyodor Dostoevsky examines in detail through the actions and lives of his characters in *Crime and Punishment*. This assignment asks you to focus on this one subject throughout the novel, annotating and taking notes on it *as you read*. It will culminate in both a presentation and an essay in which you synthesize your findings and your own ideas about that subject. This unit will take a total of roughly eight weeks.

Requirements

Each of you must, while reading *Crime and Punishment*:

- Choose from the topics listed below and write a thoughtful reflection (not more than a page) about your interest in this subject and your knowledge about it.

- Turn the subject into a guiding question that you will consider as you read and examine in the subsequent presentation and final paper; also, generate a list of questions about your topic to help you think about this subject.

- Investigate your subject online using Google, Wikipedia, the Stanford Encyclopedia of Philosophy, or other such sources. Print out evidence of what you read (e.g., the first page of a longer article that shows the title, source, subject) and add to your bibliography.

- Respond to these readings and incorporate your response to them into your final paper.

- Organize an online discussion group (through School Loop) that includes those who are investigating that same subject and contribute to the discussion at least *once* a week. As evidence of your participation, print them out and include your contributions to these discussions in the final paper.

- Annotate your copy of the text by underlining key passages and making notes in the margins. (Read with a pencil *not* a highlighter!)

- Participate in both full-class and small-group discussions about your topic.

- Write a paper (5–8 pages) in which you synthesize what Dostoevsky says and what you have learned about this subject, drawing from your notes, annotations, and reading to support and illustrate your ideas.

- Submit a bibliography of all articles, websites, and related sources (MLA format).

The Topics

Although each of the following subjects is distinct, they often share common ground. Regardless of the topic you choose, consider the subject from as many sides as possible while reading and thinking about it. You should also consider possible dimensions, such as gender, values, ethics, and age, that might apply to each topic.

- Relationships
- Choices
- Faith
- Philosophy: existentialism, utilitarianism, nihilism, Nietzsche's "Superman"
- Psychology
- Social sciences: economics, sociology, political science
  - Status
  - Class
  - Values
- Law (Justice)

Figure 2.1

Assignment Checklist

❑ **Written reflection on topic**: Why you chose this topic, what you know or want to know about it.

❑ **List of questions**: Your guiding question (the big question you will keep in mind and try to answer by book's end) and a list of at least ten other questions to help you define, apply, analyze, and evaluate ideas and events related to your subject. Examples of such questions might include:

  • What role does faith play in one's life?

  • What do a person's choices reveal about one's character and values?

  • Do all laws apply to everyone—or are there people to whom the laws do not apply?

❑ **Printouts from pages** you read about your subject on Google, Wikipedia, the Stanford Encyclopedia of Philosophy, or other such credible sources. Must include the source, first page, and author (if available).

❑ **Response to readings (Google, etc.),** in which you relate them to the novel, your own ideas, and the world in which we live.

❑ **Printouts of your contributions** to the online discussions (through School Loop) at least *once* a week.

❑ **Annotations in your copy of the novel**. These include underlining key passages, asking questions, and making notes in the margins. (Read with a pencil, *not* a highlighter!) If you cannot write in your copy, use sticky notes. I will evaluate these notes at the end of the unit.

❑ **Participation in both full-class and small-group discussions** about your topic.

❑ **Group presentation** about your selected topic in which you create some sort of experience (for example, a seminar, forum, conversation, other intellectual activity) that allows you to synthesize your own thoughts about this subject and that challenges others to do the same as a result of your presentation. (This serves as a form of prewriting for the paper you will then write.)

❑ **Paper** (5–8 pages) in which you synthesize what Dostoevsky says and what you learned about this subject, drawing from your notes, annotations, and reading to support and illustrate your ideas.

❑ **Bibliography** of all articles, websites, and related sources (MLA format).

Figure 2.2 Sample assignment checklist

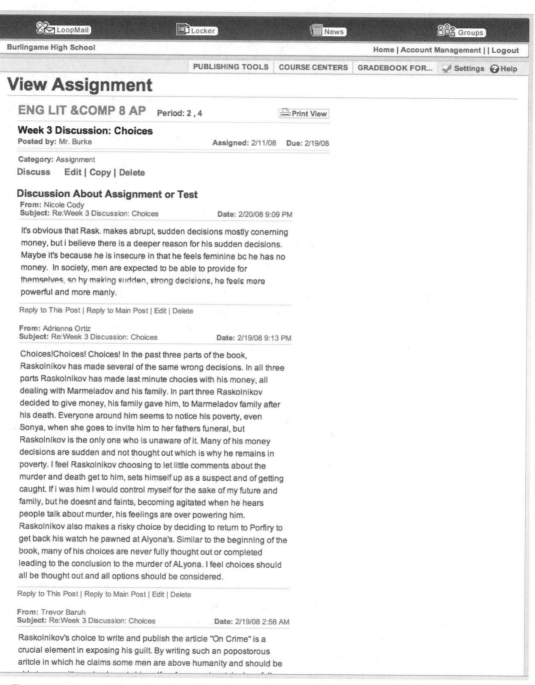

Figure 2.3 For more information about this student network system, which we use at our school, visit www.schoolloop.com.

Figure 2.2 handout), which allows me to set up a protected discussion. As you will see in the next unit, though, it is easy to do this for free, using more public forums, such as Blogger, which is available through Google.

The screenshot shows you what it looks like but gives you no sense of the discussion going on between students (from several different classes simultaneously) about the subject of, for example, choices. The following is a sample excerpt from the group investigating choices and how we make them.

From: Nicole Cody
Subject: Week 3 Discussion: Choices
Date: 2/20/08 9:09 PM

It's obvious that Rask[olnikov] makes abrupt, sudden decisions mostly concerning money, but I believe there is a deeper reason for his sudden decisions. Maybe it's because he is insecure in that he feels feminine b/c he has no money. In society, men are expected to be able to provide for themselves, so by making sudden, strong decisions, he feels more powerful and more manly.

From: Adrianna Ortiz
Subject: Week 3 Discussion: Choices
Date: 2/19/08 9:13 PM

Choices! Choices! Choices! In the past three parts of the book, Raskolnikov has made several of the same wrong decisions. In all three parts Raskolnikov has made last minute choices with his money, all dealing with Marmeladov and his family. In part three Raskolnikov decided to give the money his family gave him to Marmeladov's family after his death. Everyone around him seems to notice his poverty, even Sonya, when she goes to invite him to her father's funeral, but Raskolnikov is the only one who is unaware of it. Many of his money decisions are sudden and not thought out which is why he remains in poverty.

I feel Raskolnikov is choosing to let little comments about the murder and death get to him. He sets himself up as a suspect and of getting caught. If I was him I would control myself for the sake of my future and family, but he doesn't and faints, becoming agitated when he hears people talk about murder, his feelings are overpowering him. Raskolnikov

also makes a risky choice by deciding to return to Porfiry to get back his watch he pawned at Alyona's. Similar to the beginning of the book, many of his choices are never fully thought out or completed, leading to the conclusion to the murder of Alyona. I feel choices should all be thought out and all options should be considered.

From: Patrick Martin
Subject: Week 3 Discussion: Choices
Date: 2/18/08 11:24 PM

At this point in the story Raz is being pulled between two choices. On one side, Raz wants to move on with his life as he tries to justify his decision to murder Alyona and Lizaveta by telling himself Alyona's life was worthless and society is better without her. His motives are further revealed in his "on crime" article with superhumans and how the law doesn't apply to them. On the other hand, Raz's conscience and moral values are catching up with him as he begins to realize that maybe he isn't a "superhuman" and finds himself facing Porfiry, contemplating whether or not to confess everything. The point when the stranger yells out to Raz, "Murderer!," helps signify that maybe Raz is not "superhuman." It is the first time in which he is directly accused and this helps lead to Raz's guilty conscious.

From: Daniel Kurzrock
Subject: Week 3 Discussion: Choices
Date: 2/18/08 5:59 PM

Rodya's article "On Crime" confirms my earlier suspicions about his motives. However, we see him struggling internally about where he fits on the spectrum of "ordinary" and "extraordinary" men. He has repeatedly debated coming forward and confessing, which suggests that at those times he believes he is the first. Choosing to confess would be a sign of guilt, which would indicate that he no longer believes to be that righteous Robin Hood, or Napoleon. However, it is clear that he also often believes himself to fall under the category of "extraordinary" men. This would mean that his act of murder would be righteous, and that he made the "right" choice in fighting for a "bigger cause." What is significant is now he is actually questioning his choice, and how to act next. We'll see what he chooses. . . .

From: Victoria Pratt
Subject: Week 3 Discussion: Choices
Date: 2/15/08 9:31 PM

In Part III, Rodia's character choices are influenced by Dunia and Pulcheria's arrival to St. Petersburg. Rodia claims that he loved his mother and sister; however, after their visits to his apartment, he doesn't understand why he has "a physical hatred for them" and his inability to "have them near" him (262). Personally, I think the crime has caused him so much guilt and anxiety that he is incapable of admitting to his mother that he is a murderer. This assumption could conclude why he easily gave up Dunia and Pulcheria's earnings to Katerina for her husband's funeral. Rodia can't bear his mother and sister's generosity so, in order to make up for his mistake, he gives the money to the Marmeladov family. After Rodia describes his reasons for giving up the money so freely, Pulcheria comments that she's sure "everything [Rodia] does is very good" (217). However the shocking part is Rodia's response, which is "Don't be too sure" along with a twisted smile (217). Not that his character isn't sinful enough, but this comeback to his mother's compliment really sent his character over the edge. I think that the presence of his family has caused Rodia to feel trapped, which is the reason for his decisions in Part III.

These online conversations quickly become an important arena for discussing and generating questions raised by the story. Of course it would be overwhelming for me if I read every word every night! Instead, I monitor the groups regularly, skimming through (without reading every single word) to see what they are saying, to evaluate the quality of the discussion. This can be done in minutes. When I find a discussion bogging down or not getting down into the heart of the subject, I post questions to clarify or challenge their thinking. Here is an example of one such post for the Choices discussion.

From Teacher: Mr. Burke
Subject: Choices
Date: 2/3/08 10:31 PM

You seem to be implying that everyone is free to choose at all times. Are there times when we are not able to choose? If so, what are they? Are all choices the same or do some have costs and implications that others do not? Are the same choices available to everyone?

In this capacity, my job is to nudge the discussion in whatever way is most useful and effective. Most of the time, I use questions because I want them to do the thinking. As an alternative, I sometimes post a passage from the novel or some other source (e.g., a critical essay, that day's newspaper, a poem that comes to mind, a quotation that challenges their thinking, or a clip from a YouTube video). On most days, the discussion in class continues online later, and questions we raised in class that morning get more carefully considered responses after time for digestion. The next day, however, in-class discussion is just as likely to be informed by questions that arose online the previous night. In this way, exploring the novel through questions about big ideas, such as free will or the role of faith, transforms the class into an extended discussion.

Yet the online component is not adequate, for it is not structured, not designed to develop the sequential thinking careful analysis requires. To accomplish such disciplined thinking, I teach the students not only to ask but also to craft different types of questions using the Types of Questions handout (Figure 1).

Figure 2.4 Brittany Martinez in a discussion about choices

Types of Questions

Students can create and respond to questions for homework or work together to develop them in class. Once students have learned to ask such questions (see the example that follows), they are ready to use them to direct the class discussion. It's important to note that students need examples, such as those provided on the Types of Questions handout, to help them formulate appropriately demanding questions. Using their questions to guide the discussion makes them responsible for what is being discussed while simultaneously teaching them how to enter into and participate in an academic discussion about complex ideas.

Using the Types of Questions handout, I can say, "Antonio, what was your inductive question about last night's reading?" Once Antonio offers his question, we can then use it as a starting point for the larger discussion we will have that period. Within the context of the discussion of their questions, I also must learn to evaluate the quality of the question and the language used to express it. When a particularly good question comes up or one that is not quite clear but shows obvious potential, we stop to examine why one is so effective or how we might refine the other to improve it. On other occasions, I may write especially good questions on butcher paper and keep a running record of these for use now and in the future. Here are three sample questions from Adriana Ortiz, a great student and the best soccer player in the county!

Factual Question: Where did Raskolnikov hide the items he stole from Alyona?

Inductive Question: Why does Raskolnikov kill Alyona?

Analytical Question: How does Dostoevsky use gender to complicate the story?

On other days, there may be particular subjects I feel they need to discuss but that they might not notice or bring up on their own in the context of their own reading. When reading *Crime and Punishment,* for example, the notion of sacrifice comes up often but not in conspicuous ways they would notice. My first question when discussing a word such as *sacrifice* is to ask what it means. We brainstorm our working definitions of the word, adding personal associations, connotations, or examples to clarify and deepen our thinking. I ask someone to look it up in the dictionary I keep handy for that purpose. Figure 2.5 shows what Brittany Martinez came up with.

Thus, when students come into class, I will use their Reader's Notebook as yet one more place to pose and respond to questions. In this case I provided the

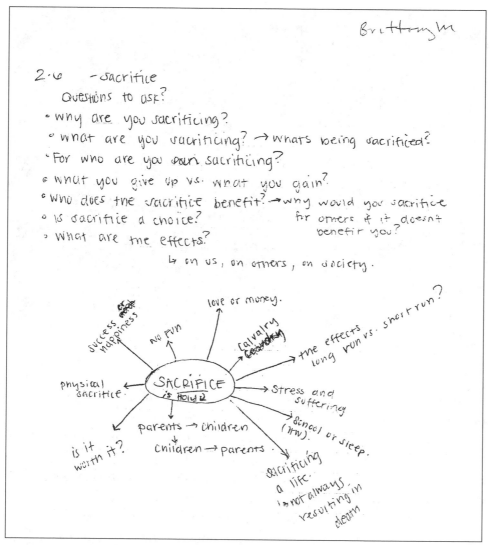

Brittany M

2·6 −sacrifice
  Questions to ask?
- why are you sacrificing?
- what are you sacrificing? → whats being sacrificed?
- For who are you own sacrificing?
- what you give up vs. what you gain?
- who does the sacrifice benefit? → why would you sacrifice for others if it doesn't benefit you?
- is sacrifice a choice?
- what are the effects?
    ⊾ on us, on others, on society.

SACRIFICE is Hard

love or money.

success happiness

No Fun

[calvary]

the effects long run vs. short run?

physical sacrifice.

Stress and suffering

parents → children
children → parents

School or sleep. (HW).

is it worth it?

sacrificing a life.

sacrificing a life. is not always resulting in death.

Figure 2.5 Brittany's *sacrifice* cluster

question ("Who sacrifices what and why?"), but note that this question is generative; that is, it is not meant to yield one answer but many. If I leave it at that, however, their thinking will be a mere list of examples of sacrifice and thus not get to the deeper levels of analysis I seek. To help them achieve that deeper level, I use a graphic organizer, a blank version of which I draw on the board to facilitate their thinking (see Figure 2.6).

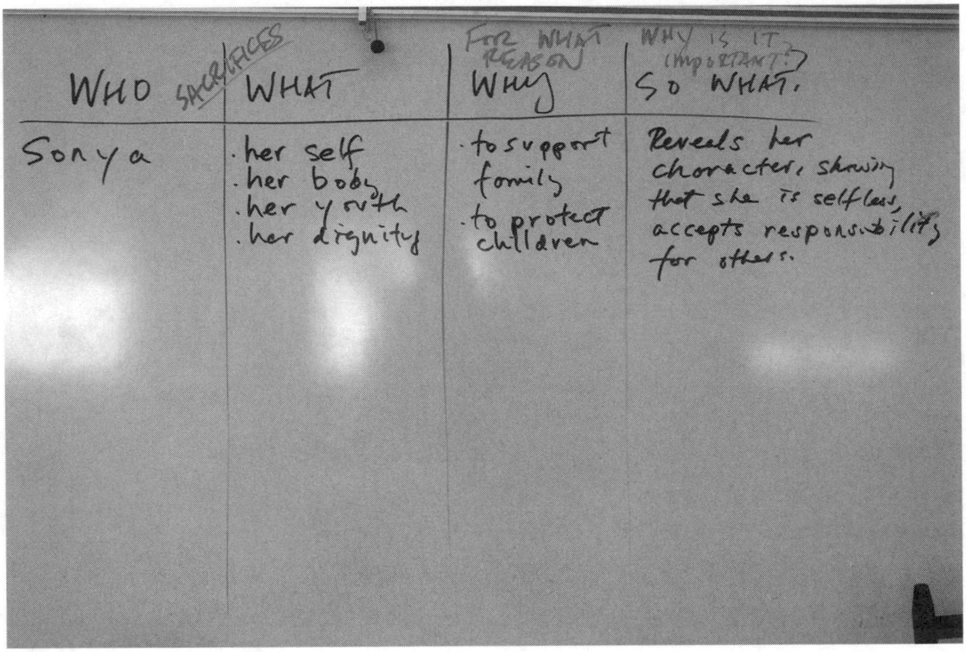

Figure 2.6 Sample of a whiteboard graphic organizer on *sacrifice*

Again, I don't want kids sitting there watching me work, looking on while I—or those five kids we all have who could talk all period—think. After first setting up the organizer on the board and modeling for them (first: I do), I then ask them to add to my first example a bit (second: *we* do); finally, they go into their notebooks and do this work on their own (third: *they* do). An example of a student's independent Reader's Notebook analysis is shown in Figure 2.7.

When they finish jotting down their own thoughts, using this organizer to generate and analyze their ideas and connections, we then use it to facilitate our subsequent discussion about *sacrifice*. As they talk, I add their ideas to the original organizer on the board, posing follow-up questions about the meaning and importance of ideas and asking for examples from the text to support what they think. While this particular organizer is helpful, others provide similar structure that develops students' analytical thinking and reading skills.

At some point, well into the novel, we feel the need for some perspective—it's a *long* book, after all—so we create a timeline. But this visual representation of the book will take us a week if we try to map out the whole book. Instead, I give

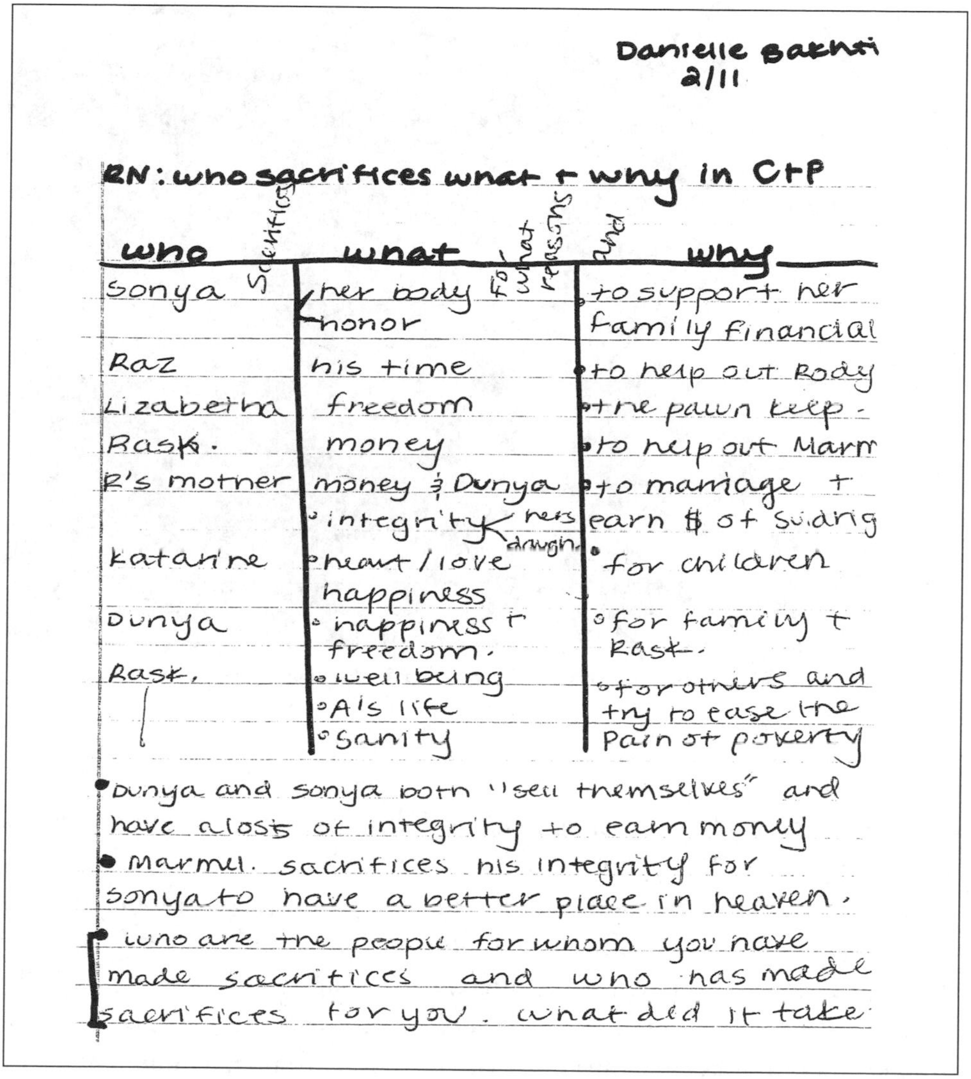

Danielle Bakhti
2/11

RN: who sacrifices what + why in C+P

who	what (sacrifices)	why (for what reasons and)
Sonya	her body, honor	to support her family financial
Raz	his time	to help out Rody
Lizabetha	freedom	the pawn keep-
Rask.	money	to help out Marm
R's mother	money & Dunya, integrity hers daughter	to marriage + earn $ of suding
Katarine	heart / love happiness	for children
Dunya	happiness + freedom.	for family + Rask.
Rask.	well being, A's life, sanity	for others and try to ease the pain of poverty

- Dunya and Sonya both "sell themselves" and have alost of integrity to earn money
- Marmel. sacrifices his integrity for Sonya to have a better place in heaven.
- who are the people for whom you have made sacrifices and who has made sacrifices for you. what did it take

Figure 2.7 Danielle's *sacrifice* chart

each student two sticky notes—one yellow, one blue—and tell them to write on the blue one *what* happened (identify a key event in their assigned section), and on the yellow *why* it is important, why it happened, and what it *means* (see Figure 4). We then use this timeline as the guiding structure for our discussion because it requires students to argue the importance and meaning of their events

Figure 2.8 Bryan and Ryan discuss where to put the event they described and analyzed before placing it on the timeline

and to provide evidence to support their assertions about the importance of these same events. (See Figure 2.8.)

Not all our thinking is done on the whiteboard or through graphic organizers. While these develop some of the more analytical and academic thinking skills, we also need to think in other directions, through other means and media. What you do, however, depends on the book you are teaching. In *Crime and Punishment*, for example, the main character's mental state and the human mind are both major aspects of the story. Abstract art offers particularly useful ways into thinking about some of these elements. Thus, on one occasion, we took time to represent, through abstract art, some idea or aspect in the novel. In the photograph shown in Figure 2.9, Travis and his group try to capture the gradual dissolution of Raskolnikov's mind-set and character through their drawing.

As students finish the novel, it is time to move toward some conclusion with the biggest book of the year. What to do? First, the question is, "What am I trying to accomplish at this point in the year?" In this case, we are fast approaching

Figure 2.9 Travis' drawing was meant to represent gradual deterioration (loss of form and structure).

spring break and winter's pale weather is a memory. To challenge them but also keep them engaged, I give them the "Teaching with Questions" assignment (Figure 2.10), which

A full-size version of this handout, customizable and reproducible, is available at www. heinemann.com.

- Allows them to work on their chosen topic (e.g., choices, faith, philosophy) in the groups they have been in for the last month

- Gives them a context in which to use all their notes on their selected topic

- Makes room for intelligent collaboration that invites creativity

- Prepares them for the final paper (on their selected topic) they will write after this assignment

In the week prior to spring break, students run their "conversations," which I have helped them shape and prepare in the previous week. In these meetings, I ask them to walk me through what they will do and why, to tell me what they think a certain activity or question will yield. I spend some of this time helping them refine questions and reorganize certain steps in ways that will achieve

Teaching the Questions

Overview

Your group is responsible for creating a conversation using some suitable approach that leads to intellectual engagement with what we will call the BQs (Big Questions). Each of you has chosen to read *Crime and Punishment* from a particular "angle of vision"—a critical perspective that interests you. Time for you to be, if not the teacher, then at least our guide, as you help us think about *Crime and Punishment* through your chosen lens.

Requirements

Each group must:

- Generate a list of possible topics from the book; these should be compelling topics that invite complex thinking and diverse perspectives. An example, for those in the Choices group, might be "the difficulty of making the right choice."
- Choose the one topic that most interests your group.
- Formulate a BQ (Big Question) based on this topic.
- Develop an effective, engaging experience or process by which you can help us explore and respond to this BQ (see Possible Ideas list below).
- Help the class make connections between your BQ and the novel (as well as your own lives and the larger world, if possible).
- Show evidence of each person's contributions through notes in the Reader's Notebook, work in the group, contributions to the actual experience you create.
- Be prepared for your group to run this discussion for *at least twenty minutes*, though it can go as long as forty-five minutes—if it's that good.

Grading

Your grade on this assignment is based on the quality of the experience you provide for the class. This experience should:

- Demonstrate the depth of your own understanding of the book and thinking about the ideas you discuss.
- Challenge us to think about a BQ that leads to new insights into the book, our own lives, and the larger world.
- Ensure the full class' participation in whatever experience you create.

Remember that the grade is collective (for the group), though I reserve the right to differentiate the grades if individuals don't demonstrate equal commitment.

Possible Ideas

Here are some ideas, though I challenge you to come up with others.

- *Socratic Seminar*: Create guiding questions you help the class explore by way of examining and responding to your BQ.
- *Visual Explanation*: Come up with some way to ask people to represent, analyze, or otherwise respond to your BQ that involves some sort of visual thinking.
- *Simulation*: Provide some experience that forces us to engage with and to explore your BQ that will get us thinking beyond the obvious yet allows everyone to connect to the novel.
- *Opinionnaire*: Create a series of questions that challenge students to think about your BQ from different angles, along a continuum, and so on.
- *Third Text*: Bring in a clip of a film, art work(s), other media, or a written text (e.g., a poem, article) that we can read quickly; use this to create a frame for a discussion through small groups and/or the full class. A variation on this would be to create a handout with quotations about your subject that students could first examine individually or in pairs or small groups. The site www.bartleby.com has several online quotation dictionaries I have found useful for this.
- *Surprise Us*. Just be sure that it makes us really think about the book and your Big Question.

Figure 2.10

more insight or greater engagement. I might suggest instructional alternatives to their proposed plan, for example:

> Instead of having the class read this article, which will take ten minutes, why don't you see what you can find on YouTube. A good two-minute clip from CNN on posttraumatic stress disorder might give you an interesting connection between Raskolnikov and people his own age today.

In other cases, I might offer a different way to do something they already had in mind:

> I like the idea of using these "What would you do?" scenarios you are planning to use. Why not write them up as a handout and add a few more of these scenarios that would test their moral boundaries, then have them talk with each other to come up with a guiding principle by which they made their choices, asking them how that compares to Raskolnikov?

After working with kids all week in these conferences—while their groups are meeting to discuss the novel—we move on to the actual presentations; in fact they are not exactly presentations but more intellectual experiences designed to both show the students' knowledge and to pass it along to others who have not read the novel through that lens. The evaluation sheet I used to assess their "Teaching with Questions" project is provided in Figure 2.12. I include the assignment requirements and grading criteria on the sheet once again so that students know what they must accomplish and I can emphasize my instructional objectives. On a more practical level, I can provide more efficient feedback if I have the criteria listed on the evaluation sheet since, in the rush of all the presentations, it is often difficult to find time to make specific notes to help students understand the grade and improve their future performances.

A full-size version of this handout, customizable and reproducible, is available at www. heinemann.com.

Whenever possible I use questions to ask students to reflect on an assignment and their performance on it. In this case, because it was a new project, I wanted seniors to not only reflect on the assignment but also to offer me feedback on how I could improve it (if they thought it was worthwhile) the following year. I consistently find that if you ask students for their feedback, they will be very helpful and specific when they know you will actually take the time to listen. Figure 2.13 shows the remarks that Matt Carruthers, a good representative of seniors at that time in the year, offered.

Figure 2.11 Brittany, Kevin, and Sarah using the overhead for a presentation.

I have but one last chance at this point to ask for a major paper—one that can serve as an intellectual rite of passage for them. It will show me what they have learned this year and themselves that they are ready to meet the demands of the colleges and universities to which they have applied (and, at this point, been accepted by). The whole unit has been designed to prepare them for this final paper: They have their notes and quotations about their subject, their guiding questions (which they can now shape into a thesis), their insights and additional textual support from their big presentations—all of which serve as prewriting for the culminating (five- to eight-page) paper.

At this point, their discussion groups become well-informed writing groups; their peers in these groups are prepared to offer more specific feedback than I probably can. For this last paper, the most demanding of the year for many of them, I want them to learn to use new aspects of the word processor, namely Track Changes (see Figure 2.14); to this end, we head into the library so that they can learn to use it according to the handout provided in Figure 2.15.

A full-size version of Figure 2.15, customizable and reproducible, is available at www. heinemann.com.

Teaching with Questions Evaluation Sheet

Topic: _____

Group Members:

1. _____

2. _____

3. _____

4. _____

5. _____

6. _____

Requirements

Each group must:

- Generate a list of possible topics from the book; these should be compelling topics that invite complex thinking and diverse perspectives.
- Choose the one topic that interests your group the most.
- Formulate a BQ based on this topic.
- Develop an effective, engaging experience or process by which you can help us explore and respond to this BQ (see list below).
- Help the class make connections between your BQ and the novel (as well as their own lives and the larger world, if possible).
- Show evidence of each person's contributions through notes in Reader's Notebook, work in the group, contributions to the actual experience you create.
- Be prepared for your group to run this discussion for *at least twenty minutes*, though it can go as long as forty-five minutes—if it's that good.

Grading

Your grade on this assignment is based on the quality of the experience you provide for the class. This experience should:

- Demonstrate the depth of your own understanding of the book and thinking about the ideas you discuss.
- Challenge us to think about a BQ that leads to new insights into the book, our own lives, and the larger world.
- Grow your participation in the group's efforts and the experience you create.

The grade is collective (for the group), although I reserve the right to differentiate the grades if individuals don't demonstrate equal contributions.

Comments

Grade

Figure 2.12

Name: MATT CARRUTHERS   Period: 2°

Crime and Punishment Presentation Evaluation

1. _8_ One a scale of 1-10, how would you rate the overall experience, as both presenter and participant, of this assignment. Explain your score briefly in the space that follows: I feel that I could have contributed more to the group, yet I feel our group was dominated by one of our team members.

2. _9_ One a scale of 1-10, to what extent did the work and discussions *within your group* help you better understand and engage with the novel? Please explain: I feel that our group's conversations & discussions went into great depth & helped me understand the mindset of Rodya better.

3. _9_ One a scale of 1-10, to what extent did the presentations/lessons *provided by your classmates* help you better understand and engage with the novel? Please explain: Every one of the other presentations were amazing. Each had a interesting discussion, concerning different aspects of the novel.

4. Please answer the following questions:

   (Y) N   Students should be encouraged to present the entire period.

   (Y) N   An entire week, with one full-period presentation a day, is valuable.

   (Y) N   Students should work on this assignment with those in their *C and P* study groups.

   (Y) N   I should have students do this assignment again next year.

Final comments about answers in #4 or in general: Encourage students next year to be more involved with going outside their comfort zones & trying new ways of presenting. Encourage the students to not only have discussions but to have activities.

Figure 2.13 Presentation evaluation completed by Matt Carruthers for *Crime and Punishment*

Figure 2.14 Students learn and practice using the Track Changes word-processing feature.

With the homestretch in mind, and the last big book of their senior year behind them, students turn in their papers, drawing this demanding unit to a close. This last paper provides both me and them a sense of accomplishment we all thought was perhaps not possible at this messy time of the year. Here is a portion of Raymond Lee's paper.

Raymond Lee
Mr. Burke
English 8 AP
4/22/08

The Choice to Fall

"If you stand up and be counted, from time to time you may get yourself knocked down. But remember this: A man flattened by an opponent can get up again. A man flattened by conformity stays down for good."

—Thomas Watson

Revising *Crime and Punishment* Papers

Burke

Guidelines

All students must do the following unless they received an A on their paper:

- Revise the paper using my comments
- Use the word-processing "Track Changes" function when making the revisions. It should look like the diagram below.
- Print and submit the page with all the changes and boxes on it.

If you do not follow these guidelines and make the changes, your grade will drop a full grade; make them, and it automatically goes up.

Papers are due when you return from spring break.

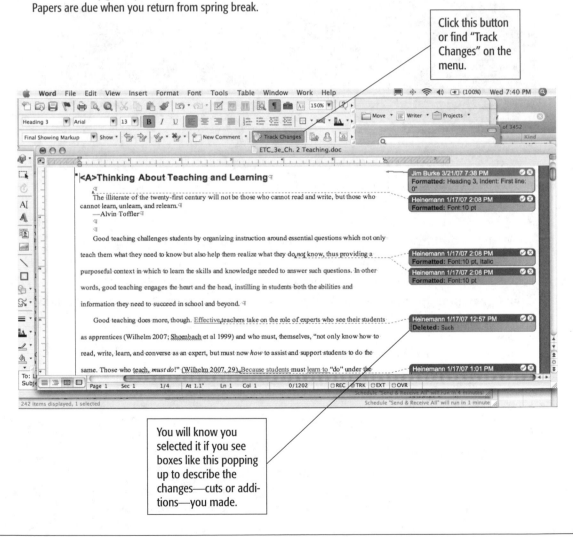

Figure 2.15 Handout for revising *Crime and Punishment* papers

The natural state of man is not to bow down and accept the rules of society, but to question them. Throughout history, man has questioned authority in the form of crime and revolution. Without these rare objections to authority, there would be no progress in society, and man would be trapped in one state of being. However, an overwhelming consenting majority combined with fear of the consequences of dissension bar most from actively questioning authority. For a few others, the fear of being "flattened by conformity" leads to an attempt at superiority over the majority. Fydor Dostoevsky's *Crime and Punishment* explores the mind of Rodya Raskolnikov, a man who spends years studying the laws that bind the common man, but wishes to achieve a greater existence above those laws. However, he becomes fixated on standing apart from the "common louse" and confuses dissension to achieve greatness with dissension to separate himself from the majority who are powerless and trapped by society. Through his exploration of Raskolnikov's philosophy and choices, Dostoevsky shows that when one deliberately aims to achieve greatness, they will inevitably suffer. Like Napoleon, being genuinely great is to rise to superiority when the opportunity presents itself, not to falsely create an opportunity to demonstrate one's greatness.

Raskolnikov strongly believes in two classes of men—the ordinary, and the extraordinary. The ordinary are trapped by the written laws of society, and have been conditioned by society to accept these decrees without question. On the other hand, the extraordinary are those who have the right to transcend written law and do as they please. Raskolnikov obsesses over discovering a reason why a man like Napoleon, who killed thousands of men, is "held sacred by society" (260) and has monuments built in his honor. He finds it remarkable that "benefactors and founders of mankind were especially terrible blood-shedders" (260). For months, Raskolnikov is consumed by the idea that crimes can benefit and advise society. However, he oversimplifies this idea, becoming fixated on the more basic idea that a criminal can be worshipped.

Through his studies of the law and those who have become "great," Raskolnikov realizes that "power is given only to the one who dares to reach down and take it...one has only to dare" (418). Raskolnikov believes that the only aspect that separates him from a Napoleon is the ability to take the initiative to stand apart. During the French Revolution, Napoleon simply needed to stand up and behead a few nobles to transcend to the savior of the common man. He brings equality to the peasants so his crimes are overlooked. Even though written law deems the revolution as treason and murder, the majority accepts it as a necessary step towards their own equality. Society as a whole wanted someone to step up and do

the dirty deed that was necessary, and that person was Napoleon. He simply needed to defy society in order to benefit it in the long run. Because the step to become superior seems so simple on paper, Raskolnikov feels he would be cheating his own potential if he did not become great. He does not want to live a hollow existence of conformity, so Raskolnikov searches for an opportunity to execute a plan to take the initiative necessary to achieve a greater existence.

In order for society to forgive his sins as it did with Napoleon, Raskolnikov must benefit the greater good through his questionable actions. Without some profit to society, a crime is just a crime that deserves punishment. To satisfy the utilitarian aspect of his philosophy, Raskolnikov chooses to kill the pawnshop owner, Alyona Ivanova, and distribute her wealth among the paupers of Russia. He sees Alyona as a minimal loss because she is a "terrible harpy" (63) in the eyes of society. She would "give four times less than [an item] is worth, and takes five or seven percent a month" (64). Alyona cheats people out of their money and is a beacon of greed in society. Raskolnikov feels that he will be morally justified in killing Alyona because he is simply ridding the world of a sinner, and will be forgiven for his own sin. He creates a façade in which he has an opportunity for himself to step up and stand apart from the common man.

Raskolnikov follows the formula he has created for greatness but after Alyona's murder, he fears society instead of making his actions known so that he can receive their praise. This was never a problem for Napoleon, however, because he already had the support of society against the nobles before he led a revolution against them. The French peasantry was already outraged at their current tax system that benefited the nobles and further impoverished the poor. Their rage creates an opportunity for Napoleon to stand up and rally the common man to create a widespread benefit in the process, even though sins would be committed in the process. By taking the initiative to help the common man when they needed it, they granted him forgiveness for any crime he would need to commit in pursuit of the greater good.

Similar to France, the proletariat of Russia was not living a luxurious lifestyle and only had enough to scrape by with the bare necessities. . . .

Raymond's essay, and those of the others, marks the transition toward the end of the year. His competency as a writer, as a reader, as a thinker—it all feels like a culmination of a year's work for us both. Along the way, however, I ask them to pause and reflect on what they are learning, what questions we are asking, and what ideas we are wrestling with and need to keep working to understand. I'm very satisfied to see Raymond's progress, no doubt about it; yet I'm equally thrilled to see what my students say they have thought about but still do not understand.

At the end of the fall semester, with a little time left in the two-hour final exam period, I asked students to answer the following questions about the fall semester:

- What was the last book you read for your independent reading?

- What question was this book trying to answer?

- What questions did we and the works we studied raise this semester?

- What are the enduring questions (i.e., those questions you feel you still need to think about) or questions we have yet to consider but that are on your mind at this point?

- What knowledge and skills do you need to further develop or acquire this next semester?

- What are your final thoughts about the fall semester?

Figure 2.16 shows what Sammy Garey had to say.

Sammy Garey

End of semester Activity:

1. I read Oryx and Crake by Margaret Atwood

2. How much can you control what happens to you? How do you deal with isolation? Why do we dwell in the past?

3. What is a leader? What makes a good leader? What is literature? What is plot? What do characters function as, and what does that show? Who am I? Am I my father's son? What is self-discovery? What is necessary to find yourself? To be, or not to be? Is there an innate darkness in all humans? If so, to what extent? How much can we control what happens to us? What is the path to darkness? What is a pilgrimage? What is justice? What is fear? Do we really have power over our fate? Who is God, what is his teaching? What is my teaching for the world? How can I live if I know I'm going to die?

4. What is love? Who am I? Am I my brother's keeper? How do I find myself? To what extent are we innately evil? How can we change our path when we feel stuck? Am I alone? DO WE REALLY HAVE CHOICES?

5. I want to develop my writing skills. I know I have come a very long way but it is entirely important to not become

Figure 2.16 Sammy Garey's reflection on questions at semester's end

stuck in my ways and to always be moving forward. Never settle! I would love the ability to continually improve.

6. I have worked so hard and I have great confidence in the progress I have made and the progress I know I will make. can't wait to get back to the grind. :)

Figure 2.16 *continued*

③ Natural Curiosity

Using Questions to Explore Relationships

Be a Columbus to whole new continents and worlds within you,
opening new channels, not of trade, but of thought.

—HENRY DAVID THOREAU, FROM "CIVIL DISOBEDIENCE"

I've taught freshman English for twenty years, at all levels, in different schools, but always freshmen. I love the mess and transition of it all. At my school, this passage from middle to high school is complicated by the fact that our freshmen come from eight different middle schools in as many different school districts since my district consists of only high schools. This means that my students bring a range of backgrounds, skill levels, academic experiences, and attitudes about school. Instead of lamenting what they cannot do or do not know, however, I prefer to think as General Washington did when, during the Revolution, someone complained about the quality of the soldiers. Washington allegedly responded, "Well, we must take them as they are and make them into the soldiers we need them to be."

While I am not trying to turn my kids into soldiers, I am very committed to shaping them into the students they need to be if they are to meet my high expectations and those of the world beyond high school. I am also intent on making them workers; that is, young adults who must face and learn to solve a range of intellectual problems so that they can be ready for the world described in a National Center on Education and the Economy report titled *Tough Choices or Tough Times* (2007):

> This is a world in which a very high level of preparation in reading, writing, speaking, mathematics, science, literature, history, and the arts will be an indispensable foundation for everything that comes after for most members of the workforce. It is a world in which comfort with ideas and abstractions is the passport to a good job, in which creativity and innovation are the key to the good life, in which high levels of education—a very different kind of education than most of us had—are going to be the only security there is. (xviii)

Before I talk about what we did and how we did it in my freshmen class, I'd like to tell you about this College Prep English class. We began the year with thirty kids, nicely divided between boys and girls. Eleven of the students were enrolled

Figure 3.1 Zac, Yaz, and Josh introduce themselves through binders, as a step toward building a strong classroom community.

in our ACCESS program for underachieving readers.* Five other students, not in the ACCESS program, had identified learning difficulties (e.g., dyslexia, language processing disorders, ADHD), and several others had often failed or otherwise struggled to succeed in years past, even though their high reading scores prevented them from being placed in the ACCESS program.

Our school uses the McDougal Littell textbook *Language of Literature*. I had never taught this particular class (nor used a textbook) before, which made it a special year for all of us: We went through it together for the first time, helping each other as we went. I began the year committed to the idea that my students could do challenging work, wrestle with big questions and complex ideas, if I guided my instruction not by the question, "How low must I go?" but, instead by,

*See my book *ACCESSing School: Teaching Struggling Readers to Achieve Academic and Personal Success* (Heinemann, 2005), which provides a detailed overview of the ACCESS program.

"What must I do to make real success a possibility for all my students without lowering my standards?" In short, I treated them as though they could learn to do everything I taught, and they pretty much did.

It was a wonderful year and, as the following pages will describe, they did substantial work. While approximately sixteen out of the twenty kids in my AC-CESS class the previous year received Ds or Fs (mostly Fs) in English, I was thrilled to find at year's end that no one failed my English class in either fall or spring. Few, I should add, received Ds, either.

Romeo and Juliet: The Big Idea

As with seemingly all freshman classes in the United States, mine are required to read *Romeo and Juliet,* an experience many in my department find frustrating since many of the incoming freshmen "read" it in middle school where their teachers wanted to "get them ready for high school–level work." Not all students actually *read* it though, do they? Yet the play is full of rich ideas, so many connections to their own lives; the question is only "Which of these gems do we choose?" Instead of reading *Romeo and Juliet* because it was required, or because it is part of the canon, or because it is about kids their age, I asked myself what questions the play asked and which ones related most to students' experience.

I very quickly realized that at the heart of the play is a question about the different relationships we have and how those relationships shape our values, actions, and lives. Thus, we used *Romeo and Juliet* to examine the question as it relates to relationships with not only friends and lovers but also mentors and authorities, enemies, and ourselves.

Jeff Wilhelm (2007) describes this approach as "reframing the existing curriculum into an inquiry unit"—an approach that he argues increases engagement, comprehension, and retention: "The research base is clear: inquiry-oriented classrooms cultivate motivation and engagement, deeper conceptual and strategic understanding, higher-level thinking, productive habits of mind, and positive attitudes toward future learning" (16).

The guiding questions about the different types of relationships and their influence on us begins long before students walk into my class to write their final exam essay on *Romeo and Juliet,* since this is the last big unit of the semester. The final will be a synthesis of all they learn in the weeks prior to that big day. When

teaching big ideas, one must begin by asking what questions a given text or topic invites one to consider and what the texts will support over the course of the unit. In addition, we need to ask what skills and knowledge this unit or text will allow us to incorporate into our instruction, as such naturally embedded academic instruction is likely to be more effective since is has a context. Thus, students come to the final exam ready to show what they know as a result of my deliberate instruction in those areas just mentioned.

INTERVIEWS: USING QUESTIONS FOR REAL LIFE

Before they even start to read the play, students investigate the relationship between two people who love each other so that they can get a sense of what that relationship is (or was) like and how it came to be. As interviews necessarily involve generating and using questions, this provides a useful context in which to teach students how to develop and pose questions that will yield useful information from those interviewed. As students often, if left unmonitored, give no thought to how to phrase questions for a particular purpose, nor when to ask a certain question (e.g., as a follow-up, to get the subject to elaborate or clarify), I created the "Interviewing: An Overview" sheet shown in Figure 3.2 for the assignment.

A full-size version of this handout, customizable and reproducible, is available at www. heinemann.com.

An assignment like this is not without its dangers and challenges, but these are important elements of any good project. I have two foster children in my class, and four others (that I *know* of) have parents going through messy, bitter divorces. A number of kids come from single-parent households. Some might even be living with relatives because their parents do not live in the country because of work or deportation. In other words, it's not a comfortable topic for many kids in the class; for some, it's not even safe. Yet education should disturb when possible; it should challenge students' perspectives, inspire curiosity, and pose questions about why things are the way they are.

Questions and ideas should, as Kafka said of literature, "be the ax that [breaks] open the frozen sea within us." For many such kids, without speaking to them directly, I suggest that they look around for someone who is obviously happily engaged or married and interview them, focusing on how this couple met and what makes their relationship so rewarding. Kids from troubled families need to see that there are other ways to live—that rich, respectful, loving relationships are possible. Of course, none of this is possible if I do not create and work hard to maintain a culture of respect and safety in my classroom; only by

Interviewing: An Overview

Mr. Burke

Overview
This assignment asks you to interview one or more people about a topic we will be discussing in class in the weeks ahead. For your interview to be successful, you must prepare for it. When you finish, you will write a short synthesis paper about what you learned.

Goals
This assignment will teach you how to:

- Generate and ask effective interview questions.
- Arrange the questions in the best order.
- Pose follow-up questions for more detailed answers.
- Take notes while others respond to your questions.
- Synthesize your notes and respond to the details in a short paper.

Step 1   Generate a list of possible people to interview for this subject. Choose the people who will give the best information and be easiest to interview.

Step 2   Make a list of questions to ask these people. The questions should all be related to the topic you are investigating and should yield *interesting* and relevant information.

Step 3   Decide which questions to ask; you should ask no more than six or seven.

Step 4   Arrange your questions in the order in which you will ask them.

Step 5   Format your note-taking page: Write your questions in the left margin, leaving room between them for answers.

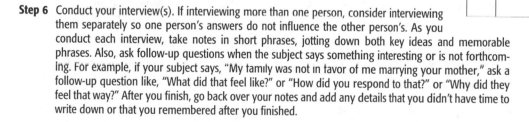

Step 6   Conduct your interview(s). If interviewing more than one person, consider interviewing them separately so one person's answers do not influence the other person's. As you conduct each interview, take notes in short phrases, jotting down both key ideas and memorable phrases. Also, ask follow-up questions when the subject says something interesting or is not forthcoming. For example, if your subject says, "My family was not in favor of me marrying your mother," ask a follow-up question like, "What did that feel like?" or "How did you respond to that?" or "Why did they feel that way?" After you finish, go back over your notes and add any details that you didn't have time to write down or that you remembered after you finished.

Remember to thank the people you interview for taking time to answer your questions!

Step 7   Write a response (1–2 pages) to the interviews, in which you synthesize (make connections between) the different details and discuss what they mean and why they are important. Include in your synthesis paper your own thoughts about what you learned from these people. What surprised you? What interested you most? Why? How do their comments correspond with what you thought *before* you interviewed them?

Figure 3.2

doing this do I show kids that such topics, while emotionally risky for them, will not require of them anything they are not comfortable doing or talking about.

The purpose of the interview is to frame the conversation about, in this case, relationships. We need some sense of what we are talking about regarding this subject, what we mean when we use certain words, and what the boundaries are when thinking about relationships. In short, it is an assignment intended to help generate ideas and connections, while also establishing some working definitions and accessing their background knowledge about the subject. Of course, it also has other, more subtle (and to me important) objectives: Teens need to talk to adults about such important subjects but don't know how or lack opportunities to have such conversations. They also need to see how what we learn in my class connects to the world in which they live and the lives of the people they know. Finally, the assignment allows me to embed certain academic essentials quietly but effectively into my curriculum: note taking, speaking and listening, evaluating, analyzing, organizing, and synthesizing.

All of these skills are evident in Alejandra's work, which begins with a list of those people she might interview and the questions she might ask them. Developing good questions is complicated and warrants the time it takes to learn how to phrase, pose, and use them. As Terry Fadem says in *The Art of Asking: Ask Better Questions, Get Better Answers* (2009), when it comes to asking questions:

> Some people are naturals, but even they need to think about improving or adding to the techniques that come easily to them. The rest of us must work at it. . . . Of course, you need to know what to ask, how to ask it, of whom and under the right circumstances. . . . "Just asking" will get "just answers." What you want are the answers you need to improve the business, solve the problem, or develop a new idea. (182)

Fadem describes in detail *twenty-five* different types of questions for a wide range of situations. In this case, however, we don't need to look at such a long list, so I have students develop the list on their own while in class. They then get into groups to grow their lists by sharing and comparing their different questions with classmates. As with most investigations, some students have never really thought about this subject and need guidance to get them going. Many, boys in particular, just don't know what questions to ask about relationships until they see some examples. Figure 3.3 shows what Alejandra came up with after first working on her own, then with a group (Figure 3.4).

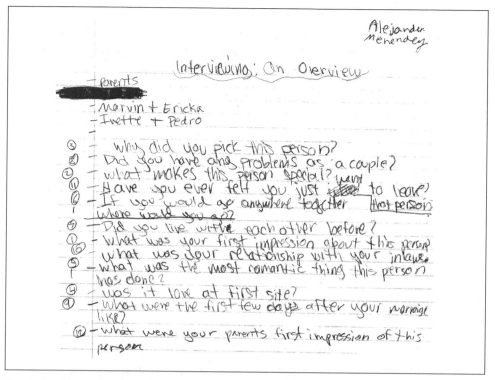

Figure 3.3 Alejandra's interview notes and questions

Figure 3.4 Alejandra and Bianca discuss their interview.

Kids often lack experience *using* questions to get information from people. They are more familiar with being peppered by questions from others: Where *were* you? Who were you *with*? What were you all *doing* there? Do you think these grades will get you into *college*, young man? You did *what*?! And so on. Fadem (2009) offers ten "basic rules" for asking questions, which we discuss in class prior to students practicing on me for a few minutes:

1. Be direct.
2. Make eye contact if asking the question in person.
3. Use plain language.
4. Use simple sentence structure.
5. Be brief.
6. Maintain focus on the subject at hand.
7. Make certain the purpose of the question is clear.
8. The question must be appropriate for the situation and the person.
9. The manner of asking should reflect the intent.
10. Know what to do with the answer. (3)

My students need some modeling and the opportunity to practice asking these questions and taking notes. To this end, after they organize their questions (note the numbers to the left of Alejandra's in Figure 3.3), I invite the class to interview me; they must take notes as they do. During the course of the interview about my relationship with my wife (which involves high school, Africa, Paris, Japan, hundreds of pages of typed letters, a house in San Francisco that her family has owned since 1918, and three wonderful children), I pause to ask how they might better phrase a question, or what some good follow-up questions would be and why they should ask them at that point. We also take time to talk about how to take notes while someone is talking; after all, I point out, you can't sit there writing away without looking at the person you are interviewing. We talk about abbreviations and acronyms, ways of creating your own shorthand, and using just one side of the page so that they can come back and supplement their notes when they have time.

By period's end, they are ready to use their questions to interview whomever they choose. Most talk to their parents, of course, but this is often the best possible result since so many do not know the story of their parents' relationship—how they met, where, when, what their life was like before kids came along. Oth-

ers now have a context and are mature enough to talk to both parents about what life was like before they got divorced, to learn that there was a time when their parents did love each other, and what led to the divorce.

Of course, sometimes kids learn unexpected and confusing things; for example, the girl who, when interviewing her parents, learned that her mother was first married to her dad's *brother* Ned ("*Uncle Ned?!* Gross! Isn't that incest!?"), but quickly realized that "it's your father (Ned's brother) I loved, so I dropped Ned and married your father and we've been happy ever since. And it's *not* incest!" I require them to interview both people in a relationship because it is sometimes amusing to find that their stories don't match up: "But dad said you met through an online dating service . . . ?"

Some kids ask if they can interview people by phone or email as one or both of their subjects are away; this is always fine and may be preferable for some since they don't have to take notes, and the online option perhaps allows for more honesty and detailed responses. Figure 3.5 shows an excerpt from Alejandra's interview of her mother.

EXTENDING QUESTIONS INTO SYNTHESIS

While I could stop at this point and call it a good assignment, the answers to the questions and the interview itself providing a nice lesson, I would miss the opportunity to have students synthesize and reflect on what they learned and how it relates to the larger questions about relationships, which the unit is designed to address. What they have really done is generated gobs of great notes and details that beg for some good writing as a way to tie it all together. Alejandra, who is in the ACCESS program, shows in the following example what students can do if they are prepared and allowed to pursue the answer to questions that interest them (even as these questions help them read Shakespeare). This reflection corresponds with Step Seven of the assignment outlined in Figure 3.2.

Reflections After Interviewing My Mother

Interviewing someone can be in many ways tough or easy. It may depend on the person. By interviewing people, you can learn a lot from them, and maybe learn their background if you are asking personal questions. It all depends on what kind of interview it is, a personal, business, or family related. I think interviews can be another way of expressing someone's

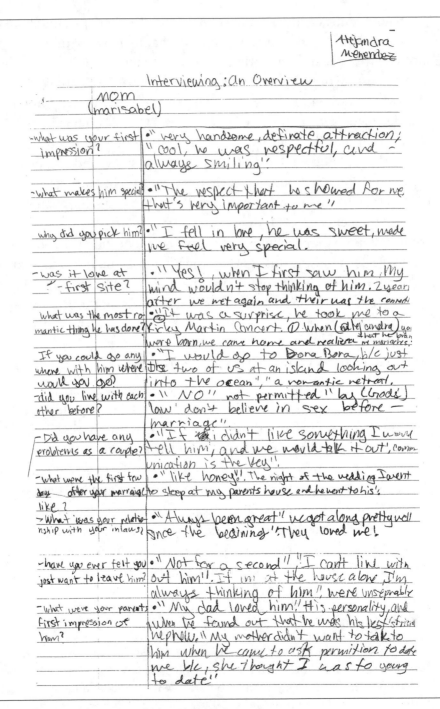

Alejandra
Menendez

Interviewing: an Overview

mom
(marisabel)

-what was your first impression?	• "very handsome, definate attraction; "cool, he was respectful, and - always smiling".
-what makes him special?	• "The respect that he showed for me, that's very important to me"
why did you pick him?	• "I fell in love, he was sweet, made me feel very special.
-was it love at -first site?	• "Yes!, when I first saw him, My mind wouldn't stop thinking of him. 2 years after we met again and their was the connect
what was the most ro- mantic thing he has done?	• "It was a surprise, he took me to a Ricky Martin concert. ① when (Alejandra) you were born, we came home and realized that he brain we mariachis.
If you could go any where with him where would you go?	• "I would go to Bora Bora, b/c just the two of us at an island looking out into the ocean", "a romantic retreat,
-did you live with each other before?	• " NO" not permitted "by (Gods) law' don't believe in sex before — marriage".
-Did you have any problems as a couple?	• "If i didn't like something I would tell him, and we would talk it out", comm- unication is the key"
-what were the first few days after your marraige like?	• "like honey". The night of the wedding I went to sleep at my parents house and he went to his.
-What was your relatio- nship with your inlaws?	• "Always been great" we got along pretty well since the beginning". They loved me!
-have you ever felt you just want to leave him?	• "Not for a second". "I cant live with out him". If im at the house alone, I'm always thinking of him". we're unseprable
-what were your parents first impression of him?	• "My dad loved him". His personality, and when he found out that he was his best friend nephew. "My mother didn't want to talk to him when he came to ask permition to date me b/c, she thought I was to young to date"

Figure 3.5 Alejandra's notes from the interview with her mother

feelings and getting to know them better. Asking my mom questions about her relationship with my dad was great. I got to know more on how she met my dad and why she picked him. While interviewing my mom it was like I was put back in time and visualized it. She made me picture the hard concrete floor of the basketball court outside her hot and humid high school and her stepping out and looking at my dad from a distance. Asking my mom what made my dad so special to her she responded, "It was the respect that he showed me, which was very important and that he was sweet, and made me feel special."

While I was interviewing my mom, I was thinking to myself that everyone always has that special someone who makes them happy, makes them laugh. They can either be a partner, family member or just a simple friend; there is always someone there for each other. What was the most romantic thing he has done was a very interesting question to me because I have always wondered if my dad was romantic at all. My mom said, "When you (Alejandra) were born, that night when you came home, I stepped into the door and started hearing this mariachi sound coming from the living room, and noticed that he had brought me a mariachi band too celebrate your birth." When I asked this question she gave me two responses that, while listening to them, I never thought my dad would do. "He also took me to Las Vegas, just the two of us, and surprised me with going to a Ricky Martin concert, which I loved!"

Interviewing is fun to me because I get to know more about the person I'm talking to and know what their opinion on things are. Also that this subject may be a bit personal, but the feeling of the trust that they give you to also talk about the subject is great.

What was very interesting to me in the interview was that whenever I asked a question, my mom never hesitated on the answer. She always new what to say and how to say it. She remembers every moment of her life with my dad, and which I think is very sweet and romantic. Some of my comments before I actually interviewed my mom were a bit different. For instance, I thought she was going to elaborate on all the questions and make them like stories each time I asked a question, but I guess I was wrong. She was very simple and straightforward but still pointed out the important things.

What surprised me when I asked this question which was, What was your parents' first impression of him?, was the answer she gave me, "My dad loved him! He loved his personality and the fact that he was his best friend's nephew. My mother on the other hand didn't really want to talk to him because when he came to my house to ask permission to date me, she thought that I was too young to date." I was surprised that my grandpa

loved him, because what I was expecting was completely different. I thought that my grandpa was going to be all protective and just give him those kinds of looks like back away. But my mom said that they loved each other, and were good friends. This taught me that anyone can be out there for someone and there will always be surprises that the end of the road for that special someone.

GRAPHIC ORGANIZERS AS A TOOL FOR EVALUATING INQUIRY

As they are conducting their interviews outside of class, we begin to move toward Shakespeare's play, stopping one last time to get them thinking about types of relationships before we read. I give them the "Conversational Roundtable" organizer, demonstrating how to use it and asking them to list the four primary relationships common to their own lives and those of the characters in the play. I then ask them to work together to develop not the types of but rather the "rules for relationships" of different types. Again, embedded in this activity are a range of important cognitive skills: generating, analyzing, organizing, evaluating, speaking, and listening.

A full-size version of the Conversational Roundtable organizer, customizable and reproducible, is available at www. heinemann.com.

What is lacking, however, is synthesis; thus, whenever I have students use such an organizing tool, I have them synthesize the ideas through a discussion, a graphic representation, an analogy, or a piece of writing. Following Figure 3.6, Alejandra's Conversational Roundtable organizer, is the written summary she used that organizer to create Figure 3.7. Note that this type of writing also creates a context in which I can introduce or reinforce important aspects of writing such as transitions, organization, classification, and subordinating conjunctions, all of which we had been studying.

While discussing these types of relationships, I ask if there are others we have ignored. Josh points out that we have not included enemies, something familiar to kids through their experiences at school and exposure to a world where the front pages of any given newspaper reminds them that countries, like people, have complex, sometimes contentious relationships. Josh's question offers an important example of the power and value of teaching through inquiry: on the way to answering one question, others arise; also, each question comes with its own assumptions, which must in turn be questioned if one is to say they fully inquired into the subject. After all, as John Stuart Mill said, "He who knows only his side of the case knows little of that" (Marinoff 2003, 185).

Name: Alejandra Menendez   Period: 1°   Date: _____

◖ Conversational Roundtable

Topic: _____

20/20 I really enjoyed your write up Alejandra! Thanks

DIRECTIONS

Ask yourself what the focus of your paper, discussion, or inquiry is. Is it a character, a theme, an idea, a trend, or a place? Then examine it from four different perspectives, or identify four different aspects of the topic. Once you have identified the four areas, find and list any appropriate quotations, examples, evidence, or details.

for doing such a great job.

1. Romantic
- be honest w/ each other
- trust each other
- love

2. Parents-child
- show respect
- get along with each other
- listen to each other

Rules for Relationships

3. Friends
- trust each other
- Loyalty
- don't fight over small things
- don't lie to each other

4. Mentor/care-taker-child
- show that you care for that person
- give advice

~~too~~ ? What were they like (marraiges/parent-child)

Figure 3.6 Alejandra's Conversational Roundtable

The types of relationships can be, all, very different. All relatio hships have rules, and decisions you have to make toge ther. While relationships that are romantic, a relationship between parents-and children have to be respectful. The romantic relationship have to have certain aspects to them. They have to be honest and loyal to each other. They don't lie and be disrespectful. The saying is children have to respect their elders and listen to them. Friends have to trust each other is for mentors to. They have to be able to talk to each other and listen if the person wants to talk, that is why relationships are very important. Which can also lead to happy lives. And relationships can also affect a life. ~~xxx~~ ~~xxx~~ While people in the 21st century marry because they meet someone and they fall in love. The connections between the couple or their relationship can affect anyone in their family or even themselves.

Figure 3.7 Alejandra's written summary of her organizer, containing her reflections on relationships

A full-size version of this handout, customizable and reproducible, is available at www. heinemann.com.

Josh's question, then, gives our good discussion about the rules of relationships (about which the kids have plenty to say) a great booster shot that sends us deeper into the subject and allows us to revisit some important ideas from earlier in the semester. I use Josh's question as a bridge back to earlier discussions about hate and as a way into the opening of *Romeo and Juliet* since the play begins by focusing, through the opening riot scene and the Prince's remarks, on hate and the violence it brings. After reading the opening scene, we use the Pyramid of Hate (see Figure 3.8), originally created to analyze genocide, to guide our examination

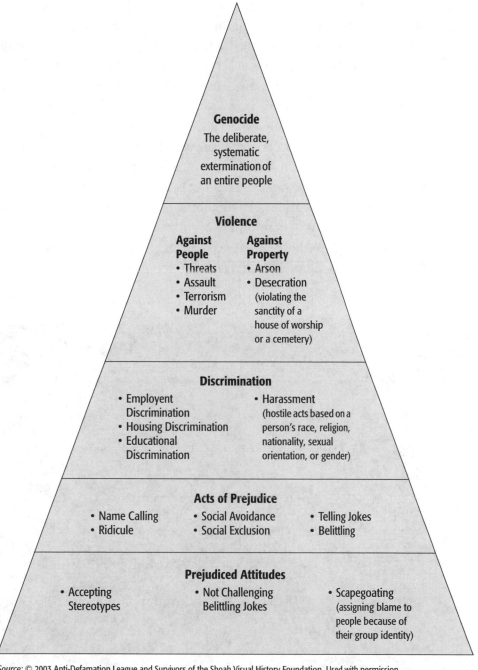

Genocide
The deliberate, systematic extermination of an entire people

Violence

Against People
- Threats
- Assault
- Terrorism
- Murder

Against Property
- Arson
- Desecration (violating the sanctity of a house of worship or a cemetery)

Discrimination
- Employent Discrimination
- Housing Discrimination
- Educational Discrimination
- Harassment (hostile acts based on a person's race, religion, nationality, sexual orientation, or gender)

Acts of Prejudice
- Name Calling
- Ridicule
- Social Avoidance
- Social Exclusion
- Telling Jokes
- Belittling

Prejudiced Attitudes
- Accepting Stereotypes
- Not Challenging Belittling Jokes
- Scapegoating (assigning blame to people because of their group identity)

Source: © 2003 Anti-Defamation League and Survivors of the Shoah Visual History Foundation. Used with permission.

Figure 3.8 The Pyramid of Hate

of how people become enemies and how such a relationship shapes our values, actions, and beliefs. To help facilitate this discussion and connect it to the larger world beyond our classroom, I invite Bruce Bramlett from SVFACES, a nonprofit organization dedicated to ending bias, discrimination, and racism, and achieving social justice and respect through its work in schools and communities, to come speak to us in class (see Figure 3.9).

Tools like the Pyramid of Hate, especially when used to connect the literature to their lives and the larger context of the world outside school, give shape to a discussion, which is important when considering complicated subjects such as relationships with one's enemies; yet, it is precisely this kind of support that allows students at all levels to get a foothold on the subject and discuss and think about it at higher levels than otherwise might be possible. The Pyramid makes an abstract concept more concrete, showing them levels, steps, and details that allow them to see how such a relation develops and could, as we know

Figure 3.9 Bruce Bramlett explains the Pyramid of Hate.

Figure 3.10 Travis works on the *Romeo and Juliet* assignment.

too well now, culminate in an attempt to destroy one's enemy and all who belong to that group.

As we move into the play, students need additional help reading it closely and connecting the play and its ideas to our Big Question. As Figure 3.11 shows, structured note taking can meet this need, providing all students the support they need for more sophisticated reading and writing about challenging texts. Note also that on such handouts I always provide examples so students know what I expect and, as mentioned before, require them to use the notes as the basis for a subsequent writing assignment; in this way they learn to synthesize the different ideas and use their notes to write.

Finally, on the last step of the assignment, students must develop an analogy, a cognitive move that asks students to consider how *x* relates to *y* (and sometimes *z*). Marzano, Pickering, and Pollock (2001) list "identifying similarities and differences" as one of nine essential teaching strategies that research supports.

A full-size version of this handout, customizable and reproducible, is available at www. heinemann.com.

Romeo and Juliet: One Love (1.1)

Step One *Reread* 1.1.170–1.1.250 specifically to understand what Romeo thinks about the subject of love. In the left column below, write down *only* quotations from this section that reflect his views about love and relationships. In the right column, write down what others, including you, think about the subject of love and relationships. Try to list your quotations and ideas using bullets.

Romeo thinks love and relationships are ...	Other people and I think ...
• "What sadness lengthens Romeo's hours? / Not having that which having makes them short" (1.1.173).	•

Step Two On the back, write a well-developed and effectively organized paragraph in which you use your notes from Step One to compare views on love and relationships. You *must* incorporate at least five quotations from the story and properly format these. Also, be sure to introduce each quotation and follow it up with some commentary.

Here is a brief and *incomplete* example:

> Romeo describes love as if it were an illness, "a madness most discrete/a choking gall, and a preserving sweet" (1.1.205) which only love can cure. This madness, however, confuses him, makes him contradict himself when he speaks of "brawling love". . . . While Romeo thinks relationships are . . . I think they are . . .

Step Three Complete the following analogy and explain your reasoning on the back:

Love is to Romeo as _____ is to _____. (Explain.)

Figure 3.11 The *Romeo and Juliet* (One Love 1.1) structured note taking handout

They describe these mental actions as "basic to human thought" and consider it the "core to all learning" (14). They elaborate on their findings, offering four key points from their research on the benefits of note taking:

- Presenting students with explicit guidance in identifying similarities and differences enhances students' understanding of and ability to use knowledge.

- Asking students to independently identify similarities and differences enhances students' understanding of and ability to use knowledge.

- Representing similarities and differences in graphic or symbolic form enhances students' understanding of and ability to use knowledge.

- Identification of similarities and differences can be accomplished in a variety of ways, four of which are "highly effective": comparing, classifying, creating metaphors, and creating analogies. (16)

In addition to identifying similarities and differences, Marzano, Pickering, and Pollock argue, based on their extensive meta-analysis of existing studies, that note taking offers significant benefits for student learning, if done in certain ways. They identify several key generalizations:

- Verbatim note taking is the least effective way to take notes as it does not allow analysis of content for importance, meaning, or connections to other material.

- Notes should be treated as work-in-progress, a draft of the emerging understanding and a document to which they should add, making additional use of them throughout the time they are studying this subject.

- The more notes taken the better as they are a valuable means for deepening students' understanding and connections throughout the learning process. (43)

Although such structured note taking is useful, it must not become repetitive or predictable, at which point students switch to cognitive autopilot and lose the benefits taking notes should have for them. After all, the final question will ask them to use the notes to consider the subject of relationships from multiple angles. With the final exam in mind, which I drafted before we began the unit, I asked the students to take notes on, for example, the relationship between Romeo and Juliet, providing an organizer specifically for that. As Figure 3.12 shows, Ilan (whose work we have already seen), despite being in the ACCESS program due to some reading difficulties, is taking detailed notes that he will

Romeo and Juliet: 2.2 (Their Relationship)   Name: Ilan Lesov

Overview We have been examining different types of relationships in the story and in our lives. In 2.1-2.2, Romeo and Juliet begin a relationship that quickly dominates their lives and clouds their thinking. This assignment asks you to try to characterize that relationship while also working on your writing skills.

Step One   Gather Details and Examples

Use the following organizer to help you find, organize, and analyze details from the text that characterize Romeo and Juliet's relationship:

What They Do or Say (quotations or examples)	What It Means (interpretation)	Why It's Important (discussion and analysis)
• "Deny they father they name"	Romance your family, leave them for me.	lack of reason
• "I would not for the would they saw thee here." (2.2.82) Romeo	• Romeo does not want anyone to see them together. Beause if someone finds out, They will both get Busted for it.	• It's hard not to see someone that you love Just because of that the fact that your families hate each other. Rome and Juliet try there hardest to overcome these 'obsticals.
• "If they do see thee, they will murder thee." (2.2.78) Romeo	• Romeo means that, if the see me with you Juliet, then they will kill me.	• Romeo and Juliet love each other uncontionaly. But since there from two sides of diffrent familes, They are not to be to-gether. That's why if someone catches them together, The will nail Romeo for it.
• "The exchange of thy love's faithful vow for mine" (2.2.138) Romeo	• Rome wants to make true Promises of love.	• Romeo want's to know that she will be only his. Noove elses. Know that she loves him, and he will love her.

Step Two   Write a Paragraph

Using the quotations and examples from Step One, write a paragraph that characterizes the relationship between Romeo and Juliet at this point. You must include at least three specific examples or quotations, (properly cited with act, scene, and line numbers). Be sure to introduce and comment on the examples/quotations before and after.

Step Three   Personal Response

Jot down your thoughts about their relationship and their actions. Do you agree with or understand what they are doing? What do you think—and why do you think it?

Figure 3.12 Ilan's *Romeo and Juliet* 2.2 (Their Relationship) handout

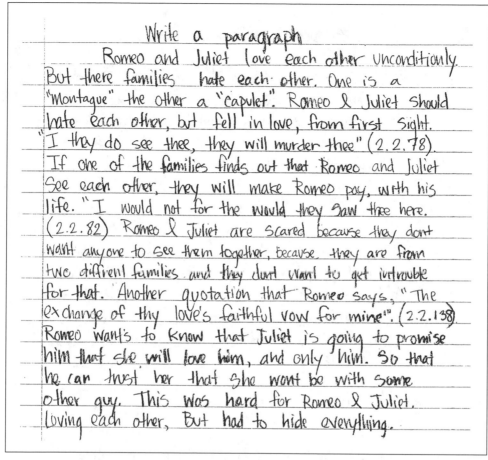

Write a paragraph

Romeo and Juliet love each other unconditionly. But there families hate each other. One is a "Montague" the other a "capulet". Romeo & Juliet should hate each other, but fell in love, from first sight. "I they do see thee, they will murder thee" (2.2.78). If one of the families finds out that Romeo and Juliet See each other, they will make Romeo pay, with his life. "I would not for the would they saw thee here. (2.2.82) Romeo & Juliet are scared because they dont want anyone to see them together, because they are from two diffrent families and they dont want to get introuble for that. Another quotation that Romeo says, "The exchange of thy love's faithful vow for mine". (2.2.138) Romeo want's to know that Juliet is going to promise him that she will love him, and only him. So that he can trust her that she wont be with some other guy. This was hard for Romeo & Juliet. Loving each other, But had to hide everything.

Figure 3.13 Ilan's *Romeo and Juliet* summary after using the handout

then use to write a response that answers the question, "How does this relate to me?" (See Figures 3.13 and 3.14.)

In addition to the previously mentioned benefits of taking notes, Marzano and his colleagues found that to be useful, notes should also be used as study guides for tests; this suggests that teachers should give serious attention not only to the content but also to the format and purpose of the notes. Throughout the Shakespeare unit, we use the notes to examine the big ideas and to prepare for the final, which in this case will be an in-class essay written on the day of the exam.

Using such note-taking assignments as a template, I can adapt them as we go along so students focus on different aspects of the story as they relate to our Big

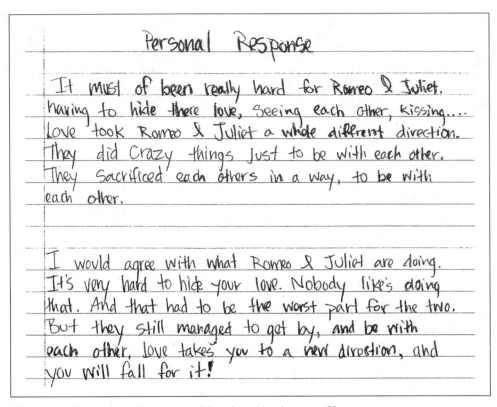

Figure 3.14 Ilan's personal response to "How does this relate to me?"

Question about relationships. I can, however, also use this flexible structure to focus on those aspects of the text that allow for meaningful connections we can explore through subsequent discussions in groups or as a class. In Figure 3.15, for example, the same assignment is revised to focus on mentoring relationships, something my freshmen already know about or need to discuss the importance of so that they can try to cultivate such relationships in their own lives.

It is in the context of such discussions that I will, for example, point out that the number one thing students in college say helped them succeed and get the most from their experience there was cultivating a lasting relationship with an adult mentor, usually a professor in their major (Light 2004). In his response, Ilan talks about the role his older brother plays in his life; he could just as easily talk about the importance of the football coaches he works with or those teachers, like myself, who see in him a young man with great potential

Romeo and Juliet: 2.3 (Mentoring Relationships)   Name: Ilan Lesov 05/12

Overview This assignment asks you to focus on the relationship between Romeo and one of his mentors, Friar Lawrence. Take notes as directed, concentrating on the nature of their relationship and how it affects Romeo.

Step One **Gather Details and Examples**

Use the following organizer to help you find, organize, and analyze details from the text that characterize Romeo and Juliet's relationship:

What They Do or Say (quotations or examples)	What It Means (interpretation)	Why It's Important (discussion and analysis)
"Retain that dear perfection which he owes without that title. Romeo, doff they name; And for they name, which is no part of thee, take all myself" (Juliet: 2.2. 48-99)	Juliet wants Romeo to remove his name because everyone in the town knows the montague & capulet families are enemies and she wants there to be no hate because of his last name.	This is important because everything would be a lot simpler if Romeo was not a part of the montague family, and this situation is affecting his and Juliet's relationship.
"So soon forsaken? young men's love then lies not truly in their hearts, but in their eyes." (Friar Lawrence: 2.3. 648)	Friar is shocked at the fact that Romeo is young, and is already in love. Friar believes that boys don't fall in love with what is inside the girl, but they fall in love with what they see on the outside.	This is important because the Friar does not understand Romeo's feelings. Friar sees this love connection between Romeo & Juliet to be childish and not last.
"Be plain, good son, and homely in thy drift; Ridding confession finds but ridding shrift." (Friar 2.3.	Friar lawrence tells Romeo that he must speak clearly or Friar will not give him the advice he needs.	This is important because if Romeo wants good advice from Friar, he must follow his direction.
"I pray thee chide me not. Her I love now doth grace for grace and love for love allow. The other did not so." (2.3	Romeo prays that Juliet will not betray him as his ex-love, Rosaline, did in the past.	This is important because it shows how much Romeo cares for Juliet

Step Two   **Write a Paragraph: One of Your Mentors**

Keep in mind the notes from above and your ideas about mentors. Write a well-developed paragraph (with great FODP) that begins with a topic sentence about one of your mentors or the role of mentors in your life. In this paragraph, discuss specific examples that illustrate how this person helps or helped you make the right decisions about life.

Step Three   **Personal Response**

Jot down your thoughts about the relationship between Romeo and Friar Lawrence. How is it similar to or different from the relationship between your mentor(s)? Provide examples and discuss them.

Figure 3.15 Ilan's work on the *Romeo and Juliet* 2.3 (Mentoring Relationships) handout

and thus take an active interest in encouraging and supporting him in his academic efforts.

Consider how much this helps students at any level, giving them structure and support, yet allowing them to consider the text at the level they can grasp while still examining the same question. In Ilan's work shown in Figures 3.16 and 3.17, see how he incorporates quotations and properly cites them, two skills we had worked on in some detail. Yet the truth is that Ilan, and everyone else in the

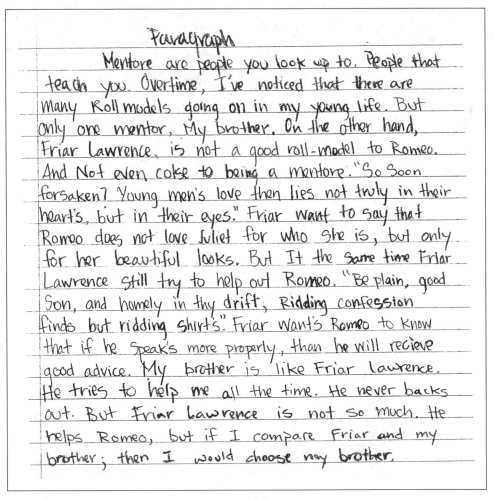

Paragraph

Mentors are people you look up to. People that teach you. Overtime, I've noticed that there are many Roll models going on in my young life. But only one mentor, My brother. On the other hand, Friar Lawrence, is not a good roll-model to Romeo. And Not even cose to being a mentore. "So soon forsaken? Young men's love then lies not truly in their heart's, but in their eyes." Friar want to say that Romeo does not love Juliet for who she is, but only for her beautiful looks. But It the same time Friar Lawrence still try to help out Romeo. "Be plain, good Son, and homely in thy drift, Ridding confession finds but ridding shirts". Friar Want's Romeo to know that if he speak's more properly, than he will recieve good advice. My brother is like Friar Lawrence. He tries to help me all the time. He never backs out. But Friar Lawrence is not so much. He helps Romeo, but if I compare Friar and my brother; then I would choose my brother.

Figure 3.16 Ilan's mentor paragraph for *Romeo and Juliet*

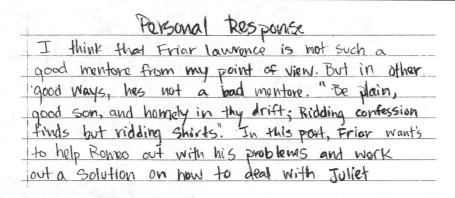

Figure 3.17 Ilan's personal response

class, will always wonder what a play like this has to do with them, a question they will never be able to answer unless we build in room for them to ask and respond to it based on their own experience (Wilhelm 2007; Smith and Wilhelm 2002; Guthrie and Wigfield 1997). Ilan's responses here and on the final exam show the difference such room for connections can make.

As we arrive at the crucial moment when Romeo and Juliet decide what to do about their love, we need a way to identify it as an important event and analyze its significance and meaning. Making decisions, something most teenagers are not so adept at doing, is worth taking time to think about because it relates to the book but also to kids' lives. After all, they face crucial and complicated questions every day but often don't realize they have options. Thus, guided by the questions, "What options does one have in a given situation?" and "How do we make the right decision?", we use the Decision Tree (see Figures 3.18 and 3.19) to help formulate responses.

First, however, we begin with students' own lives and the questions they find themselves struggling to answer: "Which classes do I take next year that will benefit me?" "Should I go away to a four-year college or stay home and go to a local community college?" "Who can I trust as my true friends?" Before we look at the choices Romeo and Juliet have, students do some writing in their notebooks about decisions they have made and the process by which they made those decisions. Then, after discussing what they wrote, we connect their experiences to

Figure 3.18 Dom works on a Decision Tree.

A full-size version
of the Decision
Tree organizer,
customizable and
reproducible, is
available at www.
heinemann.com.

the play, using the Decision Tree to structure our answers to the question, "What
are the choices they have?"

After working independently, we build a Decision Tree together on the board,
then use this diagram to facilitate our full-class discussion. I fill it in, asking questions to clarify and get them to elaborate on their thinking as we go. Throughout
this instructional sequence, we employ two key strategies that help students
meet the challenges of thinking about big ideas: asking questions and using
graphic organizers. In their analysis of research on questions, Marzano, Pickering, and Pollock (2001) describe questions as a way "that a classroom teacher
helps students use what they already know about a topic" (112), which honors
students' knowledge while also recognizing that they need to build on and learn
to better use it when thinking about new ideas and subjects. They go on to emphasize the extent to which questions are "at the heart of classroom practice . . .
account[ing] for as much as 80 percent of what occurs in a given classroom on a

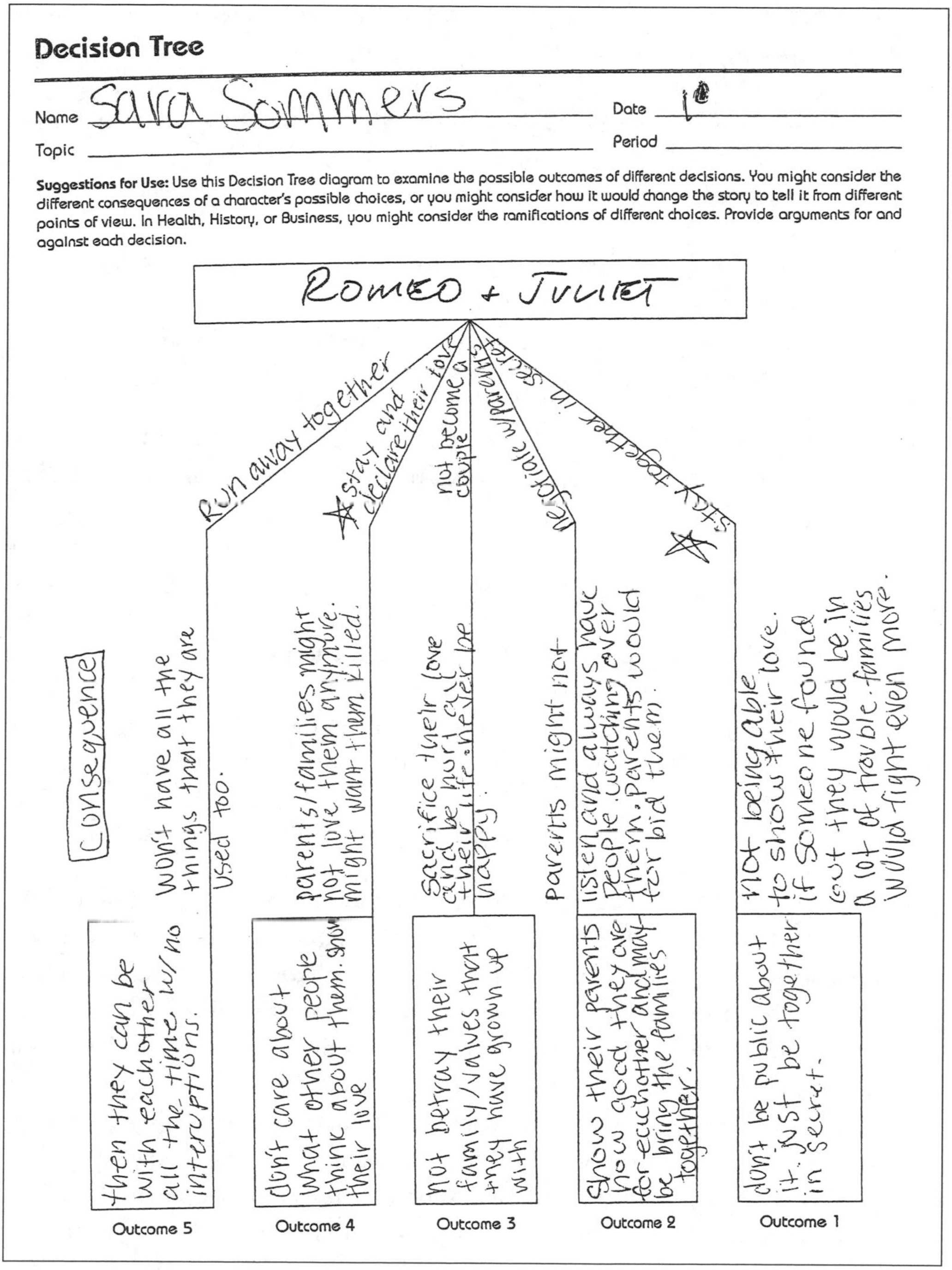

Decision Tree

Name Sara Sommers

Date 1

Topic

Period

Suggestions for Use: Use this Decision Tree diagram to examine the possible outcomes of different decisions. You might consider the different consequences of a character's possible choices, or you might consider how it would change the story to tell it from different points of view. In Health, History, or Business, you might consider the ramifications of different choices. Provide arguments for and against each decision.

ROMEO + JULIET

Run away together

☆ stay and declare their love

not become a couple

Negotiate w/parents

☆ stay together in secret

Consequence

Won't have all the things that they are used too.

parents/families might not love them anymore. might want them killed.

Sacrifice their love and be hurt or their life. wheter be happy.

Parents might not listen and always have people watching over them. Parents would for bid them.

not being able to show their love. if someone found out they would be in a lot of trouble. families would fight even more.

then they can be with eachother all the time. w/no interuptions.

don't care about what other people think about them. show their love

Not betray their family/values that they have grown up with

Show their parents how good they are for eachother and may be bring the families together.

don't be public about it. just be together in secret.

Outcome 5

Outcome 4

Outcome 3

Outcome 2

Outcome 1

Figure 3.19 Sara Sommer's completed Decision Tree

given day" (113). They conclude that there are several generalizations for the effective use of questions:

1. Cues and questions should focus on what is important as opposed to what is unusual.
2. "Higher-level" questions produce deeper learning than "lower-level" questions.
3. "Waiting" briefly before accepting responses from students has the effect of increasing the depth of students' answers.
4. Questions are effective learning tools even when asked before a learning experience. (114)

As for graphic organizers, Marzano and his colleagues identify four ideas to keep in mind when creating or using them. He refers to them as "advance organizers":

1. Advance organizers should focus on what is important as opposed to what is unusual.
2. "Higher-level" advanced organizers produce deeper learning than the "lower-level" advance organizers.
3. Advance organizers are most useful with information that is not well organized [as this allows students to use them to analyze and organize information].
4. Different types of advance organizers produce different results. (118)

Different types of organizers—expository, narrative, skimming, and illustrated—all prove effective, but Marzano, Pickering, and Pollock concluded that expository organizers achieved the greatest effect in student learning and performance. The examples provided here would fall into the illustrated organizer type, which Hyerle (1996) argues allows students to "construct a representation of knowledge" (11) and thereby enhances students' ability when it comes to "constructing and remembering, communicating and negotiating meanings, and assessing and reforming the shifting terrain of interrelated knowledge" (11).

We return to this visual representation on the board (see Figure 3.20) and use it to help us think about other decisions later in the play as a way of considering it and these decisions in a larger context. On a subsequent occasion, stu-

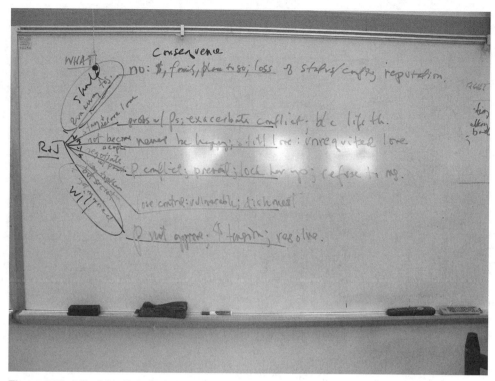

Figure 3.20 A Decision Tree on the board

dents completed a Decision Chart (Figure 3.21) that asked them to answer the questions, "What key choices did people make throughout the story?", "How important is each decision?", and "Which decision is the most important?" They then had to defend their argument as to the most important decision a character (or couple) makes. As Emily's example (Figure 3.22) shows (through the annotations), I use such an assignment to introduce or reinforce the elements of effective argument, asking students to label the different elements after they write it.

And so we read our way through the play, marching up to the day of the final on which they can use these different notes and the text to help them show what they have learned about reading, writing, and thinking. Their final exam is shown in Figure 3.23 exactly as I gave it to them. I should add that I gave this handout to them roughly a week before the final. I learned early on in the year

A full-size version of this handout, customizable and reproducible, is available at www. heinemann.com.

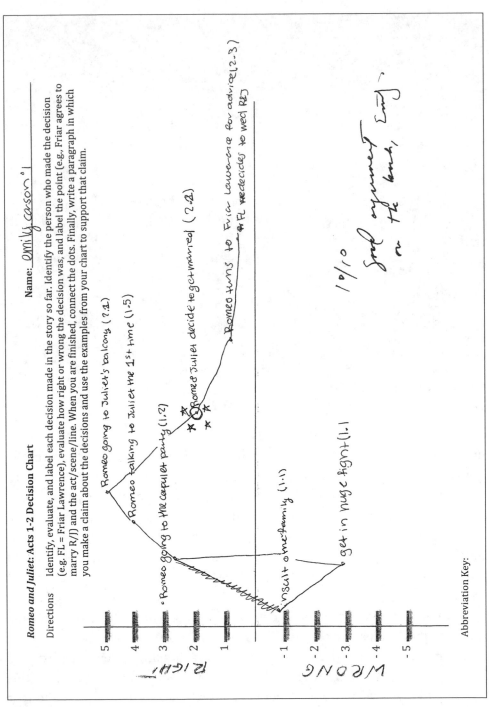

Figure 3.21 Emily Carson's Decision Chart

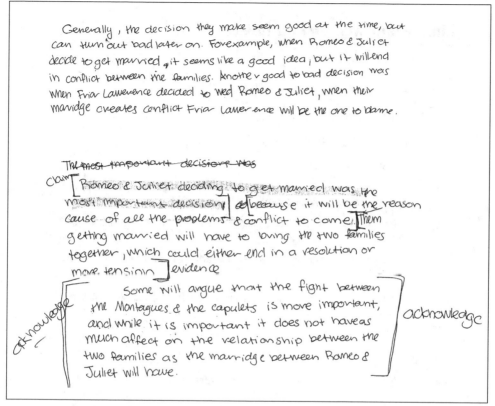

Generally, the decision they make seem good at the time, but can turn out bad later on. For example, when Romeo & Juliet decide to get married, it seems like a good idea, but it will end in conflict between the families. Another good to bad decision was when Friar Lawerence decided to wed Romeo & Juliet, when their marridge creates conflict Friar Lawerence will be the one to blame.

The ~~most important decisions was~~

Claim [Romeo & Juliet deciding to get married was the ~~most important decision~~ ot because it will be the reason cause of all the ~~problems~~ & conflict to come. Them getting married will have to bring the two families together, which could either end in a resolution or more tension] evidence

acknowledge [Some will argue that the fight between the Montegues & the capulets is more important, and while it is important it does not have as much affect on the relationship between the two families as the marridge between Romeo & Juliet will have.] acknowledge

Figure 3.22 Emily Carson's claim and discussion about decisions in *Romeo and Juliet*

that if they could prepare, if they knew what to expect, they could succeed; in this way, the final (or any other exam) was about their knowledge and skills as opposed to their ability to think quickly and show how well they can take a test on a topic (or in response to questions on an exam) they had never seen and would not think about again once they turned in that same exam.

My freshmen students arrive the day of the final, the last day of the semester, having taken finals for the prior three days. They are tired. Summer awaits them on the other side of my final exam. They can feel it and, thanks to those who have no more finals and are yelling their joy outside our window, can actually hear it; still, they have that one last final, and a demanding one: mine. The essays that follow represent only half of the two-hour final (the other half, explained further on, is about their independent reading). We had spent weeks reading the play

Final Exam: *Romeo and Juliet*

Overview
You have one hour to write an essay that shows you have:

- Completed and understood *Romeo and Juliet*

- Learned and can use FODP by including in each essay:

  - **Focus:** A clear, compelling claim about the subject

  - **Organization:** Organize ideas into and within paragraphs using transition words and other organizational strategies we have studied (e.g., compare/contrast)

  - **Development:** Examples, quotations, and explanation of their meaning and importance

  - **Purpose:** Specific purpose you are trying to achieve in each paper and within each paragraph

- Learned to properly choose, introduce, comment on, format, and cite quotations to support and illustrate your ideas.

Preparation
You are allowed to use the notes you have taken as we read and your copy of the play.

Prompt
Romeo and Juliet: Analyzing the Role of Relationships in Life and Literature

- Write an essay in which you discuss the following types of relationships in relation to life in general and *Romeo and Juliet* in particular: romantic partner/spouse, friends (best friend and regular friends), mentor(s), authorities, parents, enemies, and yourself.

- Make sure your paper and each paragraph show good FODP about these different types of relationships.

- Include examples and quotations from *Romeo and Juliet* as well as from life in general to support and illustrate the points you want to make about each type of relationship.

Figure 3.23

closely; taking notes such as those we have already seen; and writing about and discussing the characters, themes, and how all this related to our question about relationships and how they influence us. Now they have one hour, using the notes they prepared prior to the final and the text, which I allow them to consult, to write that final paper.

Student Work

Two examples follow: one by Ilan, whom we have already met and some of whose work on the play we have already seen; the second is by Jeanette Zaragoza, a very soft-spoken girl who made great progress in my class and ended by achieving great success after dedicating herself to improving the quality of her work.

As I mentioned before, family is very important to Ilan, and we see this near the end of his essay (Figure 3.24). While his essay lacks the greater structure and focus on the actual prompt that Jeanette's paper shows, his essay shows real understanding and means something to him. He is responding to the question we have been discussing and here shares his response to it, couching his examination of relationships in *Romeo and Juliet* even as he makes important personal connections to his own experience with different types of relationships (romantic, familial, paternal).

While Ilan shows that he understands key ideas about and certainly read *Romeo and Juliet*, his essay lacks in important areas that Jeanette's essay does not, no doubt a consequence of writing under pressure about a difficult text and topic. Measured against what he might do on an essay that asked him to analyze the playwright's use of imagery related to the sky throughout the play, however, I can't help but consider Ilan's essay an effective assessment of his knowledge and abilities at year's end. Jeanette, on the other hand, adhered to the prompt with greater success, organizing her essay to great effect around the types of relationships we studied, and illustrating not only her understanding of the play and ideas in it but also her abilities as a writer at the year's end (Figure 3.25). Again, it's worth reminding you that these are essays written in class, under the pressure of time. Given the chance to revise, I know both would do even better.

*A very thoughtful essay, Ilan:
much more to say, but an impressive start*

Romeo & Juliet

Ilan
05/29

Romeo and Juliet can Relate to my life when I was dating a black girl. My parents alway taught me that everything should be divided equaly. No matter what color you are or religion. Every thing and everyone should be treated the same.

I could Relate Romeo & Juliet with myself because my life with simmiler to their life, Even though Romeo was a white man, and Juliet was white lady, it was still hard to keep their relationship a secret. Juliets parents did not want Juliet to see Rome because he was the families enemie. But in my relationship with the black girl was diffrent too. When I first told my mom about my new girlfriend, and the color she was, she had this look in her face that was not too happy. But this girl and I, had a lot in common. We really liked each other. We loved spending time together and laughing it up. But my parents did not want me to have a relationship with this girl. So we had to hid our relationships. I never told my parents that I would go see this girl and had to keep it a big secret. "If They do see thee, they will murder thee." Romeo said. In this quote, Romeo Told Juliet that we have to hide when we are together. Same thing was with my girlfriend. We could of not been seen.

During this time I had my brother. He was my mentor. When I opend up to him about this, he was on myside and supported me. He told me that As long as I am happy, he will always support me. But At the same time, my brother was sure if I was Ready to be in love. Like Friar Lawrence, "So soon forsaken? Young men's love then lies not truly in their hearts, but in their eyes" (Friar: 23. My brother did not know if I was ready.

And he did not know if I really liked her heart or not.

But in the end, our relationship faded away. It was Really hard for us to be together and hide our love for each other. So we faded away. We still talk as friend and care for each other, but not as we were before.

Figure 3.24 Ilan's *Romeo and Juliet* final essay

Jeanette Zaragoza
5-29

Well
done, Jeanette!

Relationships

There are many different kinds of relationships throughout the world that guide us through our good and bad times. For example, there are relationships such as romantic, friends, mentors, parents, enemies, and even to oneself. In Romeo and Juliet there are many relationships shown throughout their life.

Relationships with our parents can be good or bad throughout our lives. Some kids are very close to their parents and feel comfortable going up to their parents for advice. Some kids on the other hand have trouble going up to their parents for advice or even just to give them a hug. In Romeo and Juliet, Juliet sees the nurse more as her mother than her own mother. Lady Capulet has trouble having a serious conversation with her daughter without the presence of the nurse. "Nurse, give leave a while, we must talk in secret. Nurse come back again; I have remembered me, thou's hear our counsel." As you can see many parents don't have close relationships with their kids which is sometimes bad because

Figure 3.25 Jeanette's *Romeo and Juliet* final essay (*continues*)

sometimes kids need the love of their family.

Relationships with friends can also be bad and good. Some people feel comfortable going up to their friends for advice than to their parents. For example, Romeo spends time with his friends for advice, especially Mercutio. They feel free to talk about anything. When Romeo was depressed about Rosaline not responding to his love, his friends convinced him to go to Juliets party. "Nay, gentle Romeo, we must have you dance." Friends can be a good guidance when confronting a depression.

Mentors are also a good way to look up to when not having anyone else to talk to or you can have more than one person to look up to, so you can have different options from different people. For example, Romeo looked up to Friar Laurence when he wanted to marry Juliet. On the way, Friar Laurence gave him advice. " For this alliance may so happy prove to turn your households' rancor to pure love. "

Good relationships with different people will guide you through challenges and struggles in your life. It is good to have ideas from different people. That way you can analyze those ideas and choose the best way to face your obstacles.

Figure 3.25 Jeanette's *Romeo and Juliet* final essay (*continued*)

Self-Selected Reading

What about the rest of the final, you may be asking. They read one self-selected book during each six-week grading period, same as the seniors, and wrote in-class essays on that book, all of which prepared them again for the final exam. It is essential to make room for such self-selected reading, for all kids need time and opportunity to explore those subjects of interest to them. In a class like my freshman English class, they need such opportunities all the more if they are to become and remain engaged readers. Ivey and Fisher (2006) found that a "majority of students cited [self-selected] reading one of the most preferred activities in an English Language Arts class" (55).

When Ivey and Fisher asked students what they like so much about time to read such books, "students consistently said that it allowed them time to think and learn" (55). To help them find the time to finish and enjoy such books, we read for the first fifteen minutes of every Tuesday and Thursday throughout the semester, during which time kids routinely lost themselves in the "reading zone" (Atwell 2007). While some kids would be reading anyway, the truth these days is that reading is a value we must cultivate and the "reading zone" is a place we need to help them learn to enter. As Atwell goes on to say of such reading,

> Selecting one's own books and having time to read them, in school and at home, aren't luxuries earned upon graduation, by virtue of surviving the curriculum. These are the wellsprings of student literacy, literary appreciation, and reading ability. Their teachers need to *expect and help* high school students to read a lot. (112)

To this end, I create, through such assignments, open-ended opportunities to read widely about a subject that interests them. Thus James, who is passionate about both soccer and his Latin American origins, can read about the lives of soccer great Pelé and his favorite revolutionary Che Guevarra. It's worth noting that James, who is in both the ACCESS class and special education program, read far more and much more challenging books thanks to the opportunity to choose his own books based on his passions (Figure 3.26).

While James read about the two fascinating men, others pursued their own interests. For example, Evan, whose passion is music, read about The Doors, Bob Marley, and The Beatles; and Nick Gee, whose interest in war led him to read different accounts of people's experiences through novels by Walter Dean Myers and nonfiction books such as *Voice of Courage* (Figure 3.27).

Figure 3.26 James Varas responds in writing to a book he is reading about Che.

Figure 3.27 Nick Gee writes about voices.

A full-size version of each of these handouts, customizable and reproducible, is available at www. heinemann.com.

Independent Reading Assignment and Student Work

Notice how the Independent Reading: Life Studies assignment handout (Figure 3.28), given at the start of the semester, allows students to frame their learning through this self-selection.

Prior to the actual in-class essay at the end of the grading period, I give them the Life Studies Essay handout that details what they must do so that they can be prepared (Figure 3.29). It is not the final essay and prompt itself; rather, the

Independent Reading: Life Studies

Mr. Burke/Spring 2009

Overview

Whereas during first semester you chose a topic and could read any kind of books you wanted to investigate it, this semester we will specifically read biographies, autobiographies, or memoirs that all have something in common. Last year, for example, one student read three biographies of influential leaders (Mao, Roosevelt, and Hitler). Another student, who loves animals and nature, read biographies or autobiographies by or about Diane Fossey, Jane Goodall, and Rachel Carson.

This semester we will choose three books that allow you to study the lives of people you find interesting and think are important. These people might be coaches, leaders in some field, historical figures, or people you respect. My hope is that you will accept this invitation to learn more about people you respect or find interesting and to learn from their lives some lessons that you can apply to your own.

Standards

This assignment meets a variety of state standards, including:

- Synthesizing content from several sources.
- Reading a wide variety of materials independently.
- Developing the main ideas of a composition through supporting evidence.
- Synthesizing information from multiple sources; identifying complexities and variations in the information and the different perspectives found in each type of source.
- Writing expository compositions and responses to literature that marshal evidence to support a thesis.
- Delivering expository presentations that include visual aids.

Requirement

This assignment asks each of you to:

- Read three books that fall into any of these categories:
  - Autobiography
  - Biography
  - Memoir
  - Nonfiction book about a team or distinct group of people (e.g., *The Nine*, by Jeffrey Toobin, about the Supreme Court justices)
- Choose books appropriate to your age and reading level. Each book should be a full-length, well-written, serious book (as opposed to a short fan biography).

Steps

Each of you must:

1. Read one of these books each grading period.
2. Bring your book every Tuesday and Thursday.
3. Come to class at the end of the grading period having finished that book and write an essay about it.
4. Give a presentation about the people you study in which you discuss their importance.
5. Write an essay at year's end that incorporates the three different books and shows your ability to write an effective essay about a subject (e.g., leadership) using details and evidence from multiple sources.

Figure 3.28

Life Studies Essay

Overview

The Life Studies assignment asked you to choose three books that allow you to study the lives of people you find interesting. These people might be coaches, leaders in some field, historical figures, or people you respect. My hope is that you have learned more about the people you respect and learned lessons from their lives that you can apply to your own. Now it's time to write!

Goals

This in-class essay has several goals. Specifically, you should:

- Establish a focus for your paper and each paragraph.

- Organize your ideas effectively to communicate them.

- Develop your ideas by providing examples and quotations, then explain how these relate to your main focus.

- Show that you read and understood the book you chose.

- Know how to properly format a bibliography for a book.

Directions

Use the following guidelines to prepare to write your essay in class on Thursday:

- Write down and properly format the bibliographic information about your book (see *Writer's Inc.* if you need more information).

- Write an introduction that tells us:
  - who this person (or group) is that you read about
  - why you read about him or her (or them)
  - what this person (or group) is known for
  - why the person (or group) is important (not just to you, but to others)

- Identify the major challenges or obstacles this person (or group) faced during life or the time you read about. Describe and discuss these challenges or obstacles in separate paragraphs. Be sure you:
  - Establish a clear and effective focus in each paragraph

    Example: Charles Schwab faced an obstacle that no one suspected and that is hard to believe: He could not read.

  - Provide examples from the book.
  - Explain how these examples relate to your main idea.

- Discuss the strategies this person (or group) used to overcome these challenges or obstacles. Be sure to include examples and to explain how these strategies helped them overcome the obstacles and eventually succeed.

- Write a concluding paragraph in which you identify and discuss those lessons you learned from this person's life and how those might relate to your own life now or in the future.

Figure 3.29

handout is designed to guide and help students prepare for the actual final, which they will not see until the day of the exam.

As students approach the end of the year and must begin to prepare for the final exam, they write an annotated bibliography about the books they have read for their Life Studies project. This allows them to synthesize the three different books while also uploading all three books back into their working memory prior to the final exam, which should include discussion of the first two books if it is to be eligible for a grade of B or higher.

Sara, the top student in the class, challenged herself at the highest levels all semester, reading three books about remarkable women (Jane Goodall, Diane Fossey, and Rachel Carson) who devoted their lives to nature; the books also provided Sara with powerful role models of women who broke through many other personal and social boundaries. Here is a sample from Sara's bibliography:

Sara Calvin
Life Studies Bibliography
Goodall, Jane. My Life with the Chimpanzees. *New York: Aladdin Paperbacks. 2002. 156 pages.*

Most people have heard of the great naturalist Jane Goodall. She is most well known for her work observing and studying the chimpanzees of Africa. However, not many know exactly what it took for her to achieve her dream of working with the primates that captured her interest and her heart. Born in London in 1934, Jane and her younger sister Judy grew up during a time of war, with Hitler taking over. As Jane grew, so did her love for animals. The animals of Africa especially interested her, and from the time she was a little girl, she knew she had to go there some day. Jane's opportunity came some time later when she was an adult, via a letter from her high school friend. Her friend's parents had purchased some property in Africa, and she wanted Jane to come visit.

After that first trip, when Jane was only 22, she continued to live her dream with the help of Louis Leakey. However, things weren't always easy. Money was a big issue; being able to save enough for her trips to Africa and back home. Also, her parents had divorced, which might not seem like it would affect her career, but it did affect her childhood. In her later years, Jane has committed herself to fighting for the rights of chimpanzees in captivity. Jane has also started a wonderful program called Roots & Shoots, which helps people do their part for nature and the environment. She is an amazing person, and I have learned from her that dreams are meant to be chased.

The day before the actual in-class essay, we use the Thesis Generator to help students develop a claim for their essays. Shannon, a student who often lacked confidence in her writing due, in part, to some learning difficulties, used the handout shown in Figure 3.30 to write her essay.

A full-size version of each of these handouts, customizable and reproducible, is available at www. heinemann.com.

Having completed these preparations, they are ready to write. Figure 3.31 shows the second part of the final exam, the prompt for the final Life Studies: Lessons on Life essay. Again, in an attempt to support all my students, they had information about the final exam well in advance so that they could prepare. Any initial reservations I had about giving my students so much lead time, so much time to prepare—"but you're giving away the keys to the kingdom!" I can imagine some thinking—disappeared once I saw how much they appreciated my commitment to support them. No one cheated; they only had the means by which to succeed.

Truly, the most transformative aspect of this year with these students was basing all my decisions on what they needed to succeed. I had no tests they could copy from, only essays they had to have done the work to write, essays they could come to class prepared to write better and thus show me more of what they had learned (and I had taught) over the course of the semester.

To illustrate the kind of work I received, I include two essays here; one is from Zac who, like Ilan, was in the ACCESS program (and achieved moderate but substantial success), and the other is from Emily, whom you've already met but whose in-class work I offer as a different measure of her success by year's end.

Zac, who had a great passion for basketball and baseball, read about the lives of people he admired who made sacrifices to become the men they did. In this context, Zac found the biographies of Michael Jordan and Kobe Bryant, as well as that of Tookie Williams (founder of the Crips gang), interesting and helpful in exploring a subject about which he had so many questions common to young men: "How can I become someone people (and I) will respect?" (See Figure 3.32.) Keep in mind that while the kids were reading these self-selected books, we were also reading others, such as *Romeo and Juliet,* required by the district.

As a student in the ACCESS program, someone for whom reading had neither been easy nor pleasurable, Zac ends the year having made real gains as both a reader and a person who had challenged himself to think deeply about questions important to him. Such reading and the questions he seeks to answer are, in their own way, a form of differentiation because Zac can choose books at his

Thesis Generator

Topic: Compare and contrast the different types of relationships humans have with nature. Include examples from your own experience and the different texts we have read or viewed. After comparing and contrasting, make a claim about what you feel are our rights and responsibilities toward the natural world in general. Provide reasons and evidence to support your claim.

Example

1. Identify the *subject* of your paper	Relationships between teenagers and their parents
2. Turn your subject into a guiding question	How does the relationship between teenagers and their parents change?
3. Answer your question with a statement	As teens grow more independent, they resent and resist the limitations and expectations their parents impose on them.
4. Refine this statement into a <u>working</u> thesis	Conflict between teenagers and their parents is a difficult but necessary stage in kids' development.

1. Identify the *subject* of your paper	~~Life Lessons~~ The story of a old man trying to figure out the lessons of Life
2. Turn your subject into a guiding question	What are the lessons of life we need to look for and learn?
3. Answer your question with a statement	By understanding that what we did in life is always done for a reason and has more meaning then we think
4. Refine this statement into a <u>working</u> thesis	There are many lessons of life that help us understand our past and future.

Figure 3.30 Shannon's Thesis Generator about lessons

Life Studies: Lessons on Life

Prompt

You read three books this semester, each one about a person's life. For the final you must write an essay in which you:

- Identify the most important lessons you learned from these books and discuss the lessons in relation to the book and your own life. This is a bit like the Angles of Vision papers you wrote for *Bless Me, Ultima* last semester. For example, you would identify a lesson you learned from one or more of your books, explain what the lesson was, how the person learned it, and how it applies to your own life.

- Gather and include evidence from the books—examples, details, quotations—to support and illustrate your claim.

- Include in your essay references to the other books, but focus on your most recent book (e.g., 70% the most recent book, 30% the other two books).

- Include in your essay a good introduction and conclusion about the lessons.

Figure 3.31

What I learned

In this semester I have read about
Stanly tookie williams, Michael Jordan, and
kobye brayant From these books I have
learned namerious things such as, how
to earn respect and work hard to get to the
top or where you want to be. One thing
I learned from tookie is that even if
your going down a wrong path it's not
to late, just as he did he was in prison
but then he almost won the nobel peace
prize. Like tookie said "If you can forgive
the past you can forgive yourself. one thing
I learned from michael's book is, working
hard and froming going to not making it
to being a legend.

In my recent book I read "koybe"
there really wasn't any struggle or tuff
decissions. Besides that he moved from his home
to a different country and came back after
7 years later. koybe pretty much had it
food. His father was also a basketball player and
was supposd to bekome better than him. when
koybe went to Morolin Highschool as a freshmen
ana was supposd to take over ammediatly
because of the arbalities he brought to the
tabel. weather it was basketball skills or his
knowledge about the game. when koybe was
a senior he was the talk of the country.
he was invited to all theese special games

picket to play in the Mcdonalds highschool
All state game, all that good stuff. But his
goal for that year was to win the state
championship, wich he thrived and attempted
to do. so when the big game came up
koybe rose above others and played like
an NBA superstar.

Figure 3.32 Zac's What I Learned essay (*continues*)

That was the next thing people were talking about "should he make the jump straight to the N.B.A." It seemed as if Koybe was ready because after highschool in the summer Koybe started praticing the the 76ers but he wasent just compeating he was dominating half the time. From there Koybe made the decesion to go the N.B.A and later le drafted by the Charolette Hornets and from there traded to the Los Angeles Lakers.

In all three books I read they all have something in common. Each person went through sacrifice to be what they are today. Tookie sacraficed his reputation to help stop some gang violence. Michael Jordan sacraficed going out with his friends and partying, but stayed home and studied and praciced everyday till there where no more fights. Yet koybe sacraficed his college oducation and risked making the wrong choice, and wind up leaving the game.

So here I am now not regreating reading thease books for it has taught me many things, such as life lessons and moral lessons. Wich seem to me to be, you need to work hard to be where you want to be, and that you should choose your own path just as you caim choose your own decisions.

Figure 3.32 Zac's What I Learned essay (*continued*)

interest and ability level, but use them to examine more ambitious questions appropriate to a fourteen-year-old boy.

Emily, on the other hand, as did many of the more high-performing students, challenged herself, reading much more adult-level books that explored her subject of the theater with greater complexity. She studied theater from three different angles—writing (Sondheim), stage acting (Anthony Rapp), and film acting (Hepburn)—and synthesized what she learned in the essay shown in Figure 3.33. These books allowed Emily to consider a range of much more

life studies   A   emily cason
°1
5|29

    After reading three books on three
very different people, I have found one
thing in common w/ all of them, despite their
rough past these people were brave enough
to carry on in life & become who they want to
be. I have from these three people that
you can't let your past interfear with who you
want to become, but insted let it help you build
who you are. Hard experiences can hurt you
and prevent you from becoming who you want
to become, but you have to take those tough
experiences and let them become a part of you.
The people in our lives, tragic events, and
learning about yourself all built our character
and make us who we are.
    The people we encounter in our lives
have a lot of influence on who we are. For
example, Stephen Sondheim's mentoring relationship
with neighbor Oscar Hammerstein II inspired
him to become who he is today. When Stephen's
parents were going thru a messy divorce he would
rush over the Hammerstein's and they would
comfort him, he was a part of their family. Oscar
taught Stephen about writing musicals when
Oscar critized stephen's first musical, "By

Figure 3.33 Emily's Life Studies essay (*continues*)

George", " in that afternoon I learned more about song writing than most people do in a life time". Not only positive relationships effect us though, Stephen had a very harsh relationship with his mother, Foxy. "All she wanted to do was get the kid out of her hair", they would always get into big fights and after Stephen would run to the Hammerstein's for comfort. Stephen wasn't a very compasonite child b/c of his mother, "even at the age of 12 he could be as bitchy as she was." Unlike Stephen, Anthony Rapp had a very close relationship w/ his mom, but she could never accept the fact that he was gay, which made him feel like he could never fully express himself.

Tragic events are what can hurt you the most, but they are also what can make you the strongest. Sondheim was clueless about his parents divorce, "suddenly there was no Daddy & an upset Mommy and you're in boarding school." Sondheim was stuck with his mom, whom he did not like. A loss is what really can change a person. When Anthony Rapp lost his mother he became much more appriciative of the relationships

Figure 3.33 Emily's Life Studies essay (*continued*)

he had w/ people. Another example is when Audrey Hepburn's father left her & her mother. It made her uncompassionate & insecure, like she couldn't love anyone. These events can change a person completley making them that way for the rest of their lives.

Learning something about yourself is another thing that can effect a person. After spending most of his time at the Hammerstein's, Stephen started to realize how much he loved musical theater and how much he wanted to be like Oscar. He "could become like Oscar w/o risking disloyalty toward his own father." After performing several years at his high school stephen started to realize that his place wasn't as an acter, but as a composer insted. These decisions changed stephen and made him who he is today.

Although these things can bring you down or make you confused they will help you out in the end. Every one has a past, without one you would n't be here or who you are. No matter how terrible your past is, you can't let it stop you from who you want to be

Figure 3.33 Emily's Life Studies essay (*continued*)

compelling, personal questions than I could have posed to her: questions about craft; process; performance; and, no doubt, happiness as it relates to what we grow up to do. Her investigation sums up the very important question of how we want to live in the world and how we become the person we dream of being.

In Their Own Words: Students' Reflections

Let me end this unit by giving the students a chance to speak in their own words. I deliberately chose to include the work of only a few kids so as to show that these assignments worked over time. We have heard from Ilan and Emily on several occasions in this unit, so it seems only fitting that we give them the last word through their year-end final reflections, which were due the day of the final exam.

What Ilan lacks in height he makes up for in muscle and speed: He was the star running back on the junior varsity football team. But he's so much more. When we had Helen Farkus, a Holocaust survivor, come to speak, he spent his own money to buy her memoir from her and stayed after to talk with her. He asked if he could read her memoir for his independent reading book, saying he didn't really like reading but found it more interesting if he could connect somehow to what he was reading. In the ACCESS class, he accepted the lessons from Ms. Hallabrin, who often shared stories with me about Ilan and the interesting questions he would ask. In short, he is an interesting kid, but also the kind of student who needs to see the relevance to his work if he is to commit to it. I could easily imagine him not doing well if he had a curriculum that did not allow for him to make the connections to his own life and the ideas that interested him. He ended the semester with a solid passing grade and a sense of pride that comes through in his portfolio cover letter, which follows.

Dear Mr. Burke,

I have not written as many essays in my entire life as I did my freshman year. And I am proud of it. I have put a lot of effort and hard work into my studies this year. Throughout the year, I have learned how to become a better writer and thinker. I would never think that I could write so many essays over a limited period of time. But now I realize how much I have

improved as a better writer, reader, and thinker. I think back on how nervous I was to write my first essay, massively. That essay was one that I was most prepared for out of all the essays I have written.

When I first came into my freshman English class, I knew that I was in the right place to be. I also noticed that you, Mr. Burke, had high expectations from your students. This is what I enjoyed this year, high expectations. These standards taught me to become a better writer. But every writer needs improvement. I will say that I can improve my FODP. I have struggled with this procedure when writing my essays. But I hope that with time, and through my next 4 years, I will end up in your AP class Mr. Burke, and show you how much I learned and improved. I have cranked it up a notch on making more sense in my essays. I have gone back and read my old essays and I am amazed on how much more interesting my writing sounds now. My most prized possessions from this year would have to be the Angles of Vision. I think that this is the best essay I have written this year because I really understood the concept of this topic. I knew where I was heading, when I was writing this essay. And plus, I got a good grade on it which should show my understanding.

Every person knows whether he or she is a good reader or not. I can tell myself that I am not the best reader. I have a little trouble with reading. For example, sometimes I need to read the directions twice to understand what it is talking about. I think that I can improve by reading more and enhancing my vocabulary. Reading books is what I love to do. If I read more books, I think that it could help me with my reading development. I have improved on understanding my reading. I have started to read more often this year. I believe that now I comprehend what I read about better than I did at the beginning of the year. Now, I am better at keeping my mind on the book that I am reading. My mind does not fade away and think about something else while I am reading a book or paper.

The best book that I have read this year was, *Remember the Holocaust* by Helen Farkas. This book helped me understand how difficult life was at this horrible period of time. When Helen came to our school and told us about her catastrophic journey to escape, it really inspired me. I realized that nothing is impossible. If you want it, than strive for excellence and you will have it no matter how hard the factor is.

Every person needs improvements. That's why next year I am going to work harder on my FODP. This is . . . what I am struggling on. And this is what I need to learn, because using FODP, is the way to write essays. I am going to read books for my summer reading. I am also going to get books to read for my own time so that I can improve my reading skills and become a better reader.

Ilan benefited from assignments that gave him a choice to explore those subjects that meant something to him, that were related to questions he sought answers to for his own reasons. Family, for example, was important to him; he often spoke and wrote about family in the books, making connections to his Russian family, particularly his older brother who was a real mentor to him. Other instructional strategies (e.g., FODP: Focus, Organization, Development, and Purpose) gave him something to hold on to, questions he could ask to generate and refine his writing. Such structures, while beneficial to all, provide extra guidance and support to a student like Ilan. Yet they also help students like Emily, whose final reflection follows.

Emily came in with great potential but struggled to handle the competing demands of high school. She won a spot in the fall musical, but a demanding rehearsal schedule and the distractions of new friends, combined with a serious workload typical of all students these days, made it difficult for her to achieve at the levels I knew she could first semester. Second semester, however, during which she could organize more of her learning around questions (related to the world of theater and acting) that engaged her, Emily gained a new focus and sustained it throughout the semester, ending with a distinguished grade. Her pride in her growth and the quality of her work is evident in her letter.

Dear Mr. Burke,

When we started in August I wasn't confident with my writing at all. I knew I could write, but my papers were unorganized and confusing. I feel that I have improved tremendously as a writer this year. I am now confident when writing my papers and I find it much easier. I also feel I have improved greatly as a reader and a thinker. I think deeper into the books I read and I am finding that I am gaining more from my reading. But, no one is a perfect writer and I still have a lot of room to improve in. I still need to work on my organizing my ideas so I can easily get my point across. I would also like to challenge myself more when I read and find books that have more depth and can make me think.

I feel that my writing has improved the most this year than all my other years. I am now confident in every paper I turn in. In the past, I struggled with organizing my ideas and my papers never had a clear point that the reader could understand; even I didn't know what my point was. I feel

that this year I am able to discover the point of my paper much easier, and people are actually able to read my paper without getting confused. I also had trouble writing introductions and conclusions. My introductions used to be long and usually gave away the whole paper and my conclusions were full of useless and usually repeated facts that loosely related to the subject of my paper.

This year I learned that you should keep your introductions short and make the reader want to keep reading and conclusions should wrap up the paper and give a "so what?" to sum up why whatever you're writing about is important. My favorite paper that I wrote this year was the Nature Essay. It was easy for me to write because I liked my topic, our effect on the animal kingdom, and I already had a lot of background information. I have felt confident in the organization and development of my ideas since learning FODP and I will keep that method with me as write even more papers and develop even more as a writer.

This year I have learned to read books that I don't necessarily want to read, but still enjoy them and find a deeper meaning that I can learn from. Before, when I read, I wouldn't dig deep for the meaning and I realized that I didn't learn from the book as much as I could have. I now ask questions and make connections while reading and I feel that I have greatly benefited from it. One book I didn't necessarily like, but I have learned a lot from this year was *Bless Me, Ultima*. If I had read it on my own, I probably would have given up by the third chapter because I didn't understand it, but I saw that if I dug deeper I would learn so much more. I also like the independent reading books I choose this and last semester. I have learned a lot not only about theater, but the people who work in it. I am excited to read more this summer using the methods of thinking I have learned this year.

This year I have learned to question and make connections in my reading and writing. I am to gain more from the books I read and write more in depth papers because of what I have learned this year. When I am writing I still feel that I need to ask more questions because no paper is ever too deep. I also need to ask more questions while I am reading because there are so many things I can learn from the books I will read in my lifetime. The biggest accomplishment I have made this year was in the independent reading books. I managed to find a connection between three very different people, Anthony Rapp, Audrey Hepburn, and Stephen Sondheim. I realized that all three of these people had several things in common that I wouldn't have realized without really thinking about the books while I read them.

Next year I hope to keep improving in reading and writing. I need to keep remembering the skills I learned this year as I continue to read more books and write more papers. I also need to keep remembering that no paper is perfect the first time you write it and to always re-write it until there are no mistakes. I am very grateful for the lessons I have learned this year and how much I have improved since the beginning of the year. This has definitely been one of my favorite English classes I have had.

Sincerely,

Emily Carson

And with those words still ringing in my ears, I locked up the classroom. Then, I headed out to the football field to watch the seniors graduate and talk to incoming freshmen whom I would see soon enough around the halls the following year. As next fall's new group enters into my class full of questions, I hope that they, like my kids this year, will still be asking those questions (along with new ones) a year later.

4 Meaningful Conversations

Essential Questions as a Way into Required Texts

It's that fundamental belief—I am my brother's keeper, I am my sister's keeper—that makes this country work. It's what allows us to pursue our individual dreams, yet still come together as a single American family. "E pluribus unum." Out of many, one.

—SENATOR BARACK OBAMA, 2004 DEMOCRATIC CONVENTION SPEECH

The previous unit showed how the year ended and everything was organized to lead up to and prepare students to succeed on the final, even as we explored these important questions about relationships. As I did in the senior unit, I want to walk through a complete unit organized around a big idea—a question we need a good chunk of time to answer or at least examine. Thus, it is important when teaching big ideas to begin with the end in mind, choosing not only a question that can sustain prolonged inquiry but also the texts, assignments, and assessments that will ensure that students learn the many different skills and gain the breadth of knowledge we expect of them during their time in our class. Yet I also want to emphasize that it is not these skills alone that matter, for if students

are not engaged in meaningful conversations, they struggle to understand and to engage with our course content.

Of Mice and Men: The Big Idea

Of Mice and Men, a book mandated by my district but which I had never taught, offered a perfect opportunity to design such a unit. This unit came near the end of the first semester, a point at which kids were getting antsy as winter break approached. We had done serious work and made real progress in the essential areas and now needed to push a bit harder, go a bit deeper, learning the strategies needed for such work as we went along. It began, however, by asking what questions this book raised that were worth spending a month thinking about. After considering different ideas, I realized that at the heart of Steinbeck's book was not just the relationship between George and Lenny, which would have allowed us to consider the nature of true friendship, but also a larger question having to do with obligation and duty. This led to the question, "Am I my brother's keeper?"—a question that has many answers, brings up cultural literacy issues (related to the Bible), and offers a rich array of texts to draw on in our discussion

Figure 4.1 Sitting with members of my freshmen class, discussing the book

of it. Of course, it also profoundly relates to the novel and gives us a useful frame-work within which to consider the story and the themes Steinbeck explores.

Before moving straight into his novel, however, students spend some time getting down their initial thoughts about this question of being a "brother's keeper." I ask them to take some time to reflect in their notebooks on what they think it means, what they think about the concept (agree? disagree?), and anything else that comes to mind. Following their written responses, we discuss what they wrote to help give us a working frame for the unit and our thinking about the ideas (see Figure 4.1). For example, Aidan wrote:

> This is a complicated idea for me because I have a brother and he doesn't always treat me the way a brother should. He puts me down all the time, never thinks anything I have to say is worth listening. So it's hard for me to think about being his "keeper" and accepting responsibility for or helping my actual brother when he doesn't do any of that for me. But he's my brother, too, so I know that if anything really serious happened he would be there for me. My friend Nate has been there for me since we were in

> kindergarten and he is much more like a brother to me than my own real brother. I'd pretty much do whatever to help out Nate. We got jumped by some guys one time coming home from school and Nate stood up for me (he's big for his age) and ever since then I have known I could always trust him. Trust, that seems like a big part of being a "brother's keeper" to me.

Such a thoughtful written response lays the foundation for an engaging, intelligent discussion. To prepare for that discussion, I ask students to underline the one line that they think best sums up their thinking about this subject. Aidan underlined his last line: "Trust, that seems like a big part of being a 'brother's keeper' to me." I then asked them to offer up their lines by way of entering into and facilitating the discussion. By doing this, I am sure everyone has something to say and I can call on and draw everyone into the discussion, even those (like Aidan) who prefer to keep to themselves.

BUILDING BACKGROUND

Before we get started reading the book, it always helps to get students warmed up. As with gardening, it helps to prepare the soil so that you can determine the conditions and supplement as needed to ensure that the plants—or, in this case, the ideas—take root and thrive. Sometimes I bring in background readings or show a video clip that helps students access or develop their background knowledge on the subject. On other occasions, we may go to the computer lab or library and spend the period doing a "quicksearch" project on topics they need to know about before reading.

In the case of *Mice and Men*, background knowledge was important since my students know so little about farming, rural life, or the experience of those who endured the Dust Bowl and Depression of the 1930s. Thus I begin by using the title to get them thinking about the book and how it might relate to the story and our question. Having established that we would be examining this question about "brother's keepers," I wrote the title on the board and worked with them to generate ideas and associations to "mice" and "men." (See Figure 4.2.)

In addition to thinking about the title and having them make predictions based on these brainstormed details, I felt that they needed some visual sense of the era and terrain since the landscape and people are so central to Steinbeck's characters. I began by using Google Earth (Figure 4.3) and the opening lines of the book to help them develop an initial sense of the landscape. Here are Steinbeck's

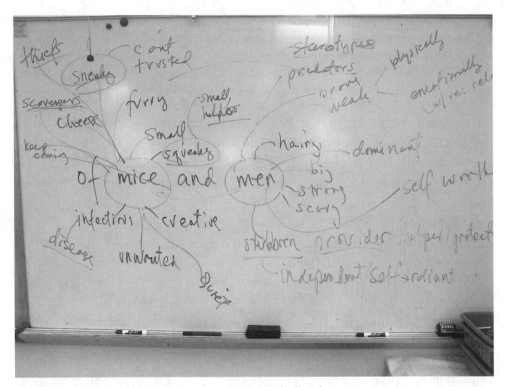

Figure 4.2 *Of Mice and Men* brainstorming summary on the board

Figure 4.3 Using Google Earth to explicate a reading

opening lines from *Mice and Men* 1937), which we read in conjunction with looking at the image of the same exact landscape on Google Earth; I project this on the
screen and annotate with my voice and fingers:

> A few miles south of Soledad, the Salinas River drops in close to the hillside
> bank and runs deep and green. The water is warm too, for it has slipped twin-
> kling over the yellow sands in the sunlight before reaching the narrow pool. On
> one side of the river the golden foothill slopes curve up to the strong and rocky
> Gabilan mountains, but on the valley side the water is lined with trees—willows
> fresh and green with every spring, carrying in their lower leaf junctures the de-
> bris of the winter's flooding; and sycamores with mottled, white, recumbent
> limbs and branches that arch over the pool. On the sandy bank under the trees
> the leaves lie deep and so crisp that a lizard makes a great skittering if he runs
> among them. Rabbits come out of the brush to sit on the sand in the evening,
> and the damp flats are covered with the night tracks of 'coons, and with the
> spread pads of dogs from the ranches, and with the split-wedge tracks of deer
> that come to drink in the dark. (1)

In addition to the images of the landscape, I want students to visualize the
people and their lives at that time. To do this, I go on Google and search for images by Dorothea Lange, the American photographer who so thoroughly docu-
mented our country and its people throughout the 1930s and 1940s with her
signature black-and-white photographs. These photographs also form a visual
corollary to our essential question, however, because the people in them are all
experiencing trials of one sort or another, most often during the Depression or
the Dust Bowl years.

Although I could just tell my students to write down whatever comes to mind
as they look at the photographs, I prefer to use each lesson as an opportunity to
incorporate as many standards and skills as possible. In this way, the lesson on
the Depression and Salinas Valley becomes a lesson on descriptive language and
reading images—in this case, photographs. Figure 4.4a shows one of Dorothy
Lange's photos, along with descriptions (Figure 4.4b) and questions (Figure 4.4c)
the class generated while discussing the photo, and a shot of one student responding (see Figure 4.4d).

One of the fundamental challenges English teachers face is how to do all
that we must within the constraints of a class period and the 180 days we have.
The Academic Essentials are those key skills and abilities all students must have

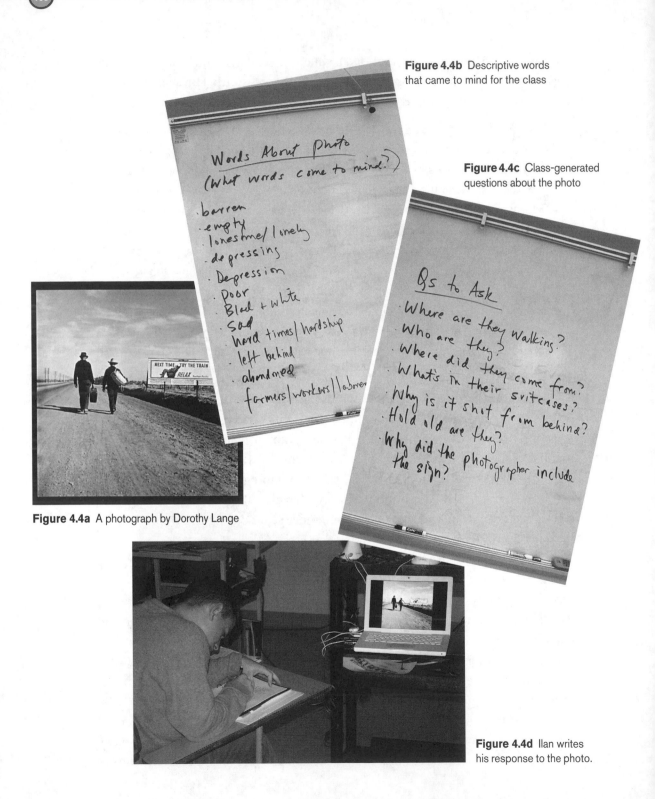

Figure 4.4b Descriptive words that came to mind for the class

Figure 4.4c Class-generated questions about the photo

Words About photo
(What words come to mind?)

· barren
· empty
· lonesome/lonely
· depressing
· Depression
· poor
· Black + white
· sad
· hard times/hardship
· left behind
· abandoned
· farmers/workers/laborers

Qs to Ask
· Where are they walking?
· Who are they?
· Where did they come from?
· What's in their suitcases?
· Why is it shot from behind?
· Hold old are they?
· Why did the photographer include the sign?

Figure 4.4a A photograph by Dorothy Lange

Figure 4.4d Ilan writes his response to the photo.

if they are to succeed in academic classes (see Appendix B). The result of careful analysis of my class and others across subject areas, the Academic Essentials offer me a useful way of designing lessons, reminding me of what I must teach students and that, like it or not, I must always try to accomplish more than one thing at a time. Thus, the Academic Essentials challenge me to integrate as much as I can within each lesson without undermining the meaning or objective of the lesson.

In this instance, my objective is to teach my students to read a range of different types of texts (in this case, photographs) and how to write with great detail, using precise vocabulary, even as we explore the concept of our responsibilities to each other. The photograph provides a context that allows me to teach them how to generate and to use questions to read different types of text, thus helping to align my instruction with the state standards without having them intrude on or otherwise undermine my curriculum.

SCAFFOLDING THINKING THROUGH QUESTIONS

Once students begin reading the book, they need a way to read purposefully that helps them comprehend the novel itself while also developing other academic essentials such as note taking and test taking. To that end, I create reading guides such as those listed in the Reading Notes in Figure 4.5. Look closely at the questions: By leading with a verb (e.g., *characterize*), I alert students to what that question focuses on; more important, I can assess my own assignment, asking myself if it is demanding enough and in the right ways. Such lead words also help to informally align my instruction with the state standards, but in a more holistic, integrated way as I look at the chapter and ask myself what aspects of it are the most appropriate to look at and develop questions about.

A full-size version of this handout (and the complete *Of Mice and Men* reading guide in Appendix A), customizable and reproducible, is available at www.heinemann.com.

Finally, the last two questions, which students must write themselves, are intended to help them develop some measure of test smarts. They create an opportunity for the students to write their own test questions, which I can then use for class discussion about not only the book but also the questions themselves. This way I can focus on why they think these are good or important questions and how they might be better phrased. This last item is important, as Langer (2002) found in her research that effective teachers embed test preparation into their instruction, making it a more authentic component of the curriculum without making it the *point* of the curriculum. (The questions shown in Figure 4.5 are just

Reading Notes for *Of Mice and Men*: Unit Two (27–37)

Introduction

While reading *Of Mice and Men,* we will pause to make some observations. These observations are intended to improve your ability to see and interpret key ideas and events in the story. Write your responses to the questions on this sheet in your Reader's Notebook *as you read*.

1. *Characterize*: Describe Curley's wife by focusing on her relationship with Curley and the men.

2. *Predict*: Based on what you know so far about Curley, his wife, and the men, what do you think will be the main conflict in the story?

3. *Connect*: What connections can you make between this story, your own life, the world in general, or other texts you have read? Explain them in detail.

4. *Connect*: How might you compare the relationship between Lennie and George and Candy and his old dog? (See page 36.)

5. *Infer*: On pages 27–37 the mood of the story changes. Generate several words to describe the mood in the story in the beginning and at the end of Chapter Two. What *causes* the change?

6. Develop two test questions based on the second chapter:

    a. **Right There (Literal) Question:** This is a factual question you can answer by pointing "right there" on the page to find the answer. An example from *The Odyssey* would be, "What test did Odysseus pass that the suitors could not?" (*Answer:* Stringing his bow and shooting the arrow through a row of ax handles.)

    b. **Between the Lines (Inferential) Question:** This question is more complex. The answer cannot be pointed to on the page but must be *inferred* from other details in the story. An example from *The Odyssey* would be, "How would you characterize the relationship between Odysseus and his men?"

Figure 4.5

a sample of the list I develop for such a novel; see Appendix A for my complete reading guide.)

Here are Justin's responses to the questions. He benefited tremendously from such structure, for he had potential but needed the support to give shape to his writing and thinking, both of which were often difficult for him.

Justin Willett
Of Mice and Men Chapter Two (27–37)

1. Curley's wife seems to be a real hand full because of the reputation she has built up around the men. The men all say the Curley's wife gives certain men the eye and freaks everybody out. They say Curley hasn't seen the eye yet but in the two weeks they have been married, she has really changed the way Curley acted around people and how he treated the men. The men all think Curley's wife is really pretty but they all know if they try to mess with her, they will get fired.

2. The main conflict of the story right now is Lennie staying out of trouble with Curley and Curley's wife. If Lennie gets into trouble, then George and Lennie will get fired and they will have no way of making money. Lennie is already really recognized around the place for not answering people when they try to talk to him so he will really have to watch out for Curley, his wife, and his father who runs the place.

3. The men in the story kind of remind me to gold miners back in the 1800 and 1900's because of the environment they are in and the problems they are having to face. This story also really relates to this story I read about this boy who ran away from home and had to survive on his own in the wilderness and face a variety of different problems he ran into on his journey.

4. Lennie and George are like brothers because of all the things that they do together. They also argue about things that are stupid and one is a more responsible person then the other. In this case George is the more responsible one because he knows all the consequences to things and realizes what they have to do to survive. Lennie is more of the worker because he is faster, smaller, and stronger then George. Candy and his old dog are just like Lennie and George because they seem to do everything together and have lived together for a very long time. Candy loves his dog and would do anything for it just like George would do anything for Lennie or vice versa.

5. In the beginning of the book, the mood was kind of slow and depressing in a way because it didn't really seem to me that there was much happening in too big of a rush. As the story progressed, it got much more exciting and interesting. The changes were caused by George and Lennie meeting new people and running into bigger problems.

6. *Right There:* How long have Curley and his wife been married so far? (Answer: Two weeks.)

7. *Between the Lines*: What do you think is going to happen to Curley's and his wife's relationship layer on in the story?

While I have given you only one sample reading guide here, the complete set of the *Of Mice and Men* guides is available in Appendix A so that you can see how they unfold and vary across the units of the book. It seems important to use such assignments as invitations to and preparations for substantial discussions in class; otherwise, the assignments run the risk of becoming "just homework" and having no actual place in the daily discourse of the class about the book itself.

In addition to the reading questions, we consider key scenes or events from different perspectives, using not only the novel but also the film to help us examine the text (see Figure 4.6). At the heart of an organizer, such as Event Notes (see Figures 4.7 and 4.8), are the questions: "Who did what to whom, why, and so what?" But another question arises, one equally important in a democratic society: "Is there another way to look at this event?"

The Event Notes organizer, adapted from the work of Linda Christensen (2000), provides the structure a student like Justin needs to be more analytical about an event, preparing him to synthesize his ideas through writing. The assignment also gives us the chance to talk about how to "read" a film, taking into consideration camera angles, characterization, staging, and mood as evoked through the music. Golden (2001) observes that

A full-size version of the Event Notes organizer, customizable and reproducible, is available at www. heinemann.com.

> . . . kids tend to be visually oriented, able to point out every significant image in a three-minute MTV music video, but when it comes to doing the same with a written text, they stare at it as if they are reading German. Nonetheless, we know, or strongly suspect, that the skills they use to decode the visual images are the same skills they use for a written text, and our goal, therefore, is to use

Figure 4.6 The class watches a scene from the movie version of *Of Mice and Men*.

that immediate interest in and uncanny ability with film and to make it work for us. (xiii)

While I am focusing here on using film *after* reading to examine an event, Golden offers an alternative worth considering under different circumstances: "We tend to read a written text and then watch its counterpart on film, but what [I am] suggesting is that we reverse the order: use a film clip to practice the reading and analytical skills that we want our students to have and *then* turn to the written text" (xiv). Before we watch the short clip of the fight scene, we brainstorm questions to ask when "reading" a film in general and this one in particular. After putting the questions on the board, we watch the excerpt, referring back to the questions to guide us in our analysis of the film and its connection to the written text.

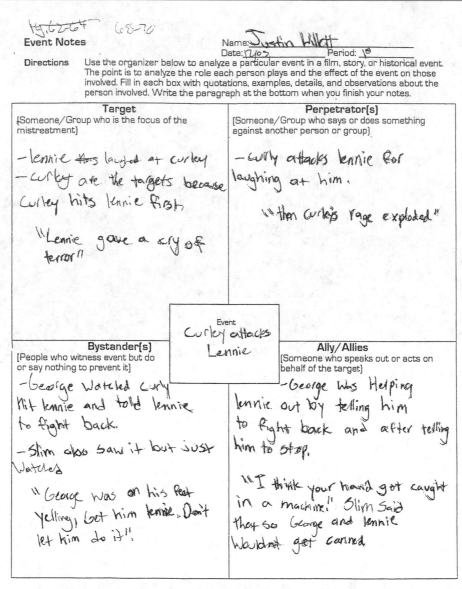

Event Notes

Name: Justin Willett

Date: 1/1/02   Period: 1°

Directions Use the organizer below to analyze a particular event in a film, story, or historical event. The point is to analyze the role each person plays and the effect of the event on those involved. Fill in each box with quotations, examples, details, and observations about the person involved. Write the paragraph at the bottom when you finish your notes.

Target
[Someone/Group who is the focus of the mistreatment]

- lennie ~~was~~ laughed at curley
- curley are the targets because curley hits lennie first

"lennie gave a cry of terror"

Perpetrator(s)
[Someone/Group who says or does something against another person or group]

- curly attacks lennie for laughing at him.

"then curley's rage exploded"

Event
Curley attacks Lennie

Bystander(s)
[People who witness event but do or say nothing to prevent it]

- George Watched curly hit lennie and told lennie to fight back.
- Slim also saw it but just watched

"George was on his feet Yelling, Get him lennie, Don't let him do it!"

Ally/Allies
[Someone who speaks out or acts on behalf of the target]

- George was Helping lennie out by telling him to fight back and after telling him to stop.

"I think your hand got caught in a machine!" Slim Said that so George and lennie wouldn't get canned.

Follow Up: Use the notes above to write a paragraph in which you make a statement about who did what to whom and why. Use examples from the text and your notes to support and illustrate your ideas. Here is a sample argument:

Frank betrayed Ahmed because he resented his success and status.

Figure 4.7 Event Notes written by Justin Willett

Figure 4.8 Yaz and Matt Smith work with a novel and the Event Notes organizer.

EXTENDING INQUIRY THROUGH SUPPLEMENTAL TEXTS

Once we are really digging into the heart of the novel, I complicate the discussion by incorporating other texts that will allow us to consider the big question about my "brother's keeper" from different perspectives; I then connect it back to the novel itself. Because we live in a visual culture, it is essential that students know how to read not only photographs but also commercials, advertisements, and films. On this occasion, I bring in an advertisement from the Red Cross (Figure 4.9) that beautifully reflects the question of our responsibility to each other. As with other texts, we begin by generating "Qs to Ask" on the board, creating a list of what to ask when reading advertisements in general and this one in particular. After discussing these, rephrasing some, and analyzing why others are so effective, the students write an analysis of the ad, explaining how it relates to the Big Question and our ongoing conversation.

In addition to the Red Cross ad, we considered the issue of gender inherent in the Big Question; to do this, I showed an image of the cover of Jodi Picoult's

Figure 4.9 Red Cross advertisement

novel *My Sister's Keeper*, I use this to broaden the discussion and reframe it as a larger question about one's obligation to any other person.

Assignments and Student Work

As we near the end of the novel, we begin to work on an essay about allies, focusing on narrative writing that also includes an analytical element about the qualities and effects of mentors. In addition to Steinbeck's novel, which we are reading as part of a conversation about our obligation to others (as opposed to reading it to read it because it is required), we start reading a collection of personal essays from *A Hand to Guide Me* (2006), a rich collection of short essays (each about five hundred words), edited by Denzel Washington as part of his work with the Boys and Girls Clubs of America. Using these essays to extend our discussion about obligation (and incorporate yet other types of texts, in this case essays), students annotate them; specifically, students must identify the author's problem and ally, then analyze how that ally helped the author. Finally, they write a summary of and response to the article. These texts offer not only inspiring stories but also models for the essay my students will write about the Ally Essay prompt shown in Figure 4.10.

The Ally Essay brought together many of the ideas we had been discussing, but it also made room for connections to their own lives, something students need if the learning is to stick. Matt Smith, a wonderful kid who often had

A full-size version of this handout, customizable and reproducible, is available at www. heinemann.com.

Ally Essay Prompt

We all have allies in our lives, people who help us achieve those goals we set for ourselves or that others have set for us. Some contribute more than others, of course. In your essay, identify one person who has been your biggest ally in one particular area—sports, school, performing arts, or some other area—or during a particular difficult period in your life. Describe what that person did and how they helped you. Provide examples and connect these examples to your main idea.

May be photocopied for classroom use. © 2010 by Jim Burke from *What's the Big Idea?* Portsmouth, NH: Heinemann

Figure 4.10

encounters with the administration, wrote about his parents, two wonderful and caring people, who adopted Matt when he was an infant. Here is his essay:

Allies Essay

It is a great blessing to have someone welcome you into their arms and accept you as one of their own and love you as if they were the ones that gave you life. It is the most amazing feeling to know they will always be there no matter what and will love you no matter what. My parents are my biggest allies, my greatest contributors, and my stability. Both my mom and my dad have made sure that I grow up the best I can. They have bailed me out of situations and let me experience life and not held me back. I could not pick just one to write about, but must tell you about both, because they are both equally important.

My father, who has been more of the discipliner, has gotten me out of a lot of bad situations. For example, at my old school, I got in trouble for being to out of control, and to unpredictable. My father went into the school and came to my defense. I don't know what he said, but if it wasn't for him then a lot of things would have been different. My father once said to me, "Matt, you can mess up a thousand times and fall, but I want you to learn from your mistakes. I will, however, be there for you to help you get up on your feet and I will never ever stop loving you, no matter what." I will never forget that. In that moment, I understood what love was, and the intensity and passion that you can have for one person. My father and I may not always get along and I may not say this to him enough, but he will always be one of my best friends and I have the deepest respect for him.

Now my mom has been more lenient but worries so much more about me. I guess in a way I'm grateful because I know that she cares and it's always good to be reminded. My mom always asks how my life is and sometime can cross her boundaries but that's only because she loves me and wants to be in it all the time. I guess I don't show her how much she means to me. One of the biggest things is that I'm grateful to have my mom for her advice. She always just tells me to take a step back and look at all of the aspects of the problem. After a couple hundred of times I finally started to incorporate taking my time and slowing down into my everyday life.

Being my mother must be a challenge and I don't make it easy for her. I'm not the most respectful, I don't always tell her how much I love her, and I get into trouble but she still loves me. I've known some mothers just to leave and abandoned there children when it gets hard but my mother never gives it up and always takes my challenges and never puts me

down. She always finds a way to make everything better. I would be a much worse person if I didn't have her.

Now when they both are together and come and talk to me about my life and struggles I refer to them as the dream team. When they both come and talk to me there's no getting out of it. My father always seems to be more of the upfront one and my mother tries to and insinuates what she wants to know or what she [wants] me to tell her. I guess the thing that just amazes me about them is that the first time they ever saw me was in the orphanage fighting a kid who's older than me. They didn't turn away, but knew I was right for them and I guess that should have been a heads up that I was a handful even though I can't remember it. I think that's where everything changed, and I'm forever in their debt.

Both of my parents are equally important to me. They have taught me life lessons like treating women right and doing what I feel is best. I will keep those lessons and many more with me the rest of my days, and that one day I hope to teach my children. Sometimes I think that I take them for granted. They have never really asked much of me just to be the same loving person they always have known. They have given so much for me and would give up their happiness for mine. That is one of the most comforting things that has been consistent throughout my whole life. No essay and no words can explain how much they mean to me and how much I love them. I only hope I will be able to do as great as job with my kids as they have done with me.

BLOGGING THE BIG IDEAS

As we approach the end of the "Brother's Keeper" unit, I find myself wondering how I might assess their understanding of the *Of Mice and Men* book and the key ideas we have discussed throughout the unit. The trick is to come up with some culminating work that everything prior has prepared the students to do but that is not redundant. Because we wrote the Ally Essay, I feel no urgent need to have students write another essay right on the heels of the multi-step process we used for that essay. Yet at the end of a book, we all feel some need to bring it all together—assess their understanding and, in my case, reflect on the Big Question one last time.

I had one last text I wanted to include in this unit but wasn't sure how to fit it in: then-Senator Barack Obama's speech at the 2004 Democratic convention in which his recurring theme was, "Am I my brother's keeper?" Still, we needed to do something more active at this point after all the hard work on the essay and

A full-size version of Figure 4.11, customizable and reproducible, is available at www. heinemann.com.

finishing up the novel. The solution was an in-class blog fest that would require them to read an excerpt from the Obama speech, respond to it, and connect it to *Of Mice and Men*. Figure 4.11 shows the assignment I came up with. Figure 4.12 shows the blog I set up using free Blogger software available through Google; it included the directions and the excerpt from Obama's speech.

I should add that online assignments like this one take us into a different compositional realm where we face the dilemma of whether to insist on correct spelling and grammar or to allow students to use the more informal (and often incorrect or unconventional) language common to online writing. I subscribe to the idea that it is a genre, a domain with its own idiosyncratic and evolving rules and ways; thus, I do not insist on "correct" writing in this context, although I confess to remaining defiantly antiquated in my continued use of capitals, correct spelling, and even apostrophes—a commitment for which I receive endless teasing from my own teenage sons.

Here are some sample responses from the period-long blog session:

Adam H said . . .

I believe that we are our brothers keeper. We are a single unit, a single country and we must help each other in order to live a great life. If one person is suffering in this country, do we just turn our head and idling stand by. Think if we were the people living without the basic necessities of life, would you want someone to help you out? Our simple acts of kindness towards each other make the world a better place. If we didn't take care of our others then things like the fight between Lenny and Curley would have gone on. Maybe there would have been a loss of life, something much more harmful then what happened. If George and the rest of the group felt that Curley got into himself and didn't help him things would have been much worse for the group. If you want to better improve your own life you have to improve the lives around you.

Justin W. said . . .

"Am I my brothers keeper" to Obama is that he doesn't like to see people who have to decide apon medication or rent. That puts him down. He dosent like to see a family who cant even aford a lawyer in a lawsuit. In the story "Of mice and men" relates to george and lennie and how close they are. They do everything with eachother and they are respectful of oneother. What if everyone in the world were all equal and all had the

Of Mice and Men Online Socratic Seminar: Am I My Brother's Keeper?

Overview: We have finished reading *Of Mice and Men* and will use this week to bring the inquiry (and the semester!) to a close. Instead of writing a paper or giving presentations, which we don't have time to do well, I thought we would combine writing and discussion by having a Socratic Seminar online. In short, a Socratic Seminar asks students to consider a subject from different perspectives, asking questions that help them and their classmates to clarify and extend their thinking about the subject they are studying.

Objectives

My intention is to use the discussion to:

- Learn how to post written responses to an online blog
- Consider a question from several different perspectives
- Pose questions to other students, the text, and the author that lead to new and deeper thinking about the subject
- Elaborate on your thinking through written discussion
- Make connections to the text, yourself, other texts, and the world
- Provide support for your ideas from the text or other reliable sources

Grading

- Your grade on this assignment will be based on the quality of your participation in class and online, as well as the quality of your work as spelled out in the Objectives section above. This is equivalent to a major assignment, so do your very best.

Step One

- Log on to the blog: http://mrburkesfreshmen.blogspot.com.
- Read the directions, including Barack Obama's remarks.
- Post a response to Obama's ideas and the question, "Am I my brother's keeper?" As part of your response, you need to connect these ideas to *Of Mice and Men* somehow, using examples from the text to develop and support your ideas. This should be a thoughtful, well-developed response, not just a couple of dashed-off sentences.

Step Two

- Read most of the other responses from your classmates on the blog.
- Post *two questions* in response to other people's posts. These questions should invite people to clarify or defend their ideas. For example, you might ask, "What if everyone did what you suggest? What would be the effect of that?" or you might ask, "How would you relate that to George's relationship with Lennie?"

Step Three

- *Respond* to at least *two* questions or postings.
- Your responses should be well developed. Use some of the sentence starters in the margin to help you get started if you are stuck.

Step Four

- Read through most of the responses, jotting down notes about big and common ideas that appear throughout the different comments.
- Write a final commentary that ties together your own thoughts and those of others, but also adds one last idea, perhaps your final thought about this subject of "my brother's keeper."
- Include in this last comment new ideas or opinions you have about this subject and what led you to these new thoughts.

SENTENCE STARTERS

Prior Knowledge
- I already know that . . .
- This relates to . . .
- This reminds me of . . .

Asking Questions
- I wonder why . . . ?
- What if . . . ?
- Why is it . . . ?

Making Connections
- That's like in the book when . . .
- That reminds me of what we studied in history: . . .
- This is similar to when . . .
- I can relate to that because . . .

Summarizing
- The main idea is . . .
- Everyone seems to think . . .
- The most important points are . . .

Comparing
- _____ is like _____ because . . .
- Steinbeck and Obama are saying the same thing: . . .
- Steinbeck and Obama agree that _____ but I think _____ would not agree about _____, because . . .

Clarifying/Revising
- What I mean is . . .
- Another way of saying this is . . .
- I didn't mean to imply _____ but then I . . .
- At first I thought _____ but then I realized _____ and now think . . .

Reflecting and Relating
- In the end, I believe . . .
- I first thought _____ but now think _____ because . . .
- While I realize _____ I think _____ because . . .
- This is relevant to my life because . . .
- My conclusion at this point is that . . .

Figure 4.11

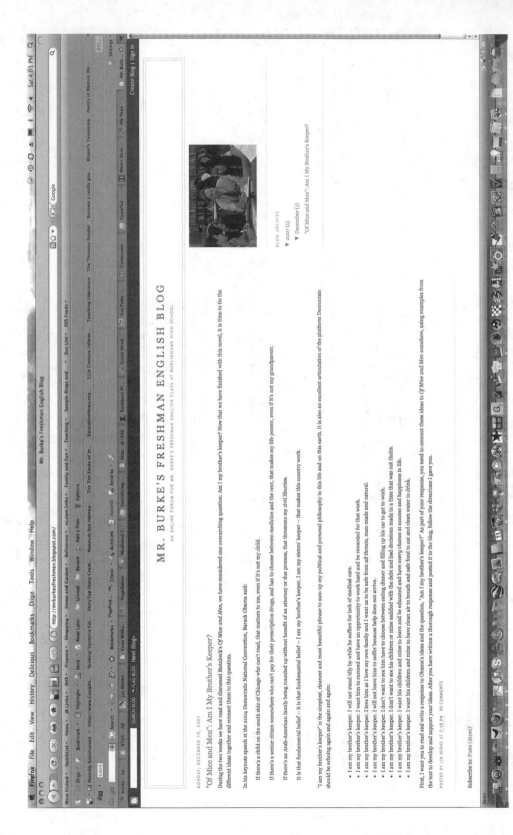

Figure 4.12 The *Of Mice and Men* freshmen blog

same amount of money and fame, would the world be the same? Everyone seems to think that people with more money, power, and fame deserve to live and enjoy life but part of what Obama say's is that everyone should care about everyone around them.

Justin Willett

Matt S. said . . .

I think that some of the statements that Barack Obama says are not all accurate or possible. Yes, you can and want to take care of your "brother" but sometimes you can't. when he says "I will not stand idly by while he suffers for lack of medical care." In some situations, many situations, your struggling paying for you own familys medical care. and no matter how hard you want to its not always possible.

That statement dose apply to george and lenny. George dose take care of lenny. but its not okay to kill another human being but maybe he did it out of love.

Figure 4.13 Sarah Calvin working on an Online Socratic Seminar blog

Saamy P. said . . .

Obama's remark, "Am I my brother's keeper," may relate to George and Lennie, but not to most of the world. Towards the end of the book George may be asking himself this question to see if he was protecting Lennie or just taking him out for his own good. However, most people in the world don't get to this point in time where they have a choice to decide between a hard life or death. For example, children in Darfur may never get a chance to eat safe food and drink clean water, which will never give their brothers the chance to live up to Obama's ideas.

Saamy Phan

It was a very intense period, one during which some students needed help learning how to blog, which was one of my objectives, and everyone had to think about the speech—about its content and how it related to the *Of Mice and Men* book and our essential question. The final result was about twenty-five pages of writing, some better than others, but all of it thoughtful. The next day I asked students several questions by way of assessing the value of the assignment and getting their feedback on how it could be improved. Here is what Alejandra wrote:

I really liked how we used the example with Barack Obama because it helped me understand *Of Mice and Men* more efficiently and in more detail. It also helped me think about it from another perspective and how George and Lennie are so close like brothers, and how they take care of each other. I think we can maybe do the blog again with other books we are going to read. It helped me realize the importance of the story and the book.

A full-size version of the Unit Planning Sheet, customizable and reproducible, is available at www. heinemann.com.

Such units require careful planning but the results suggest they are worth it. In subsequent units (remember, the *Of Mice and Men* unit was first semester), I started creating one-page unit planning sheets like the one in Figure 4.14 for a second-semester unit on nature. (See Appendix E for a blank version of this planning sheet.) The *Of Mice and Men* unit resulted in many rich discussions, but it also allowed me to teach students and reinforce what they already knew about the Academic Essentials.

Unit Plan: Our Place in Nature

Big Idea   What are our rights and responsibilities as they relate to the natural world?

Reading	Writing	Speaking	Investigations	Misc.
• SS: "Brothers Are the Same," by Markham	• RN: What animal would you be or are you most like?	Socratic seminars on topic and texts	Quicksearch project(s) in iMac lab or library on zoos and other topics	**Language Study** • G: Clauses/phrases through sentence modeling, combining • Voc: misc.
• SS: "My Wonder Horse"	• RN: McDonough quotation: explain and respond	Class discussions	YouTube search for videos on nature	
• NF: from *Caged Bird*, by Angelou	• P: Position paper on zoos	Small-group discussions	Interviews about the Big Idea and other topics (zoo)	
• P: "Traveling Thru Dark," by Stafford	• RN: Response to zoo articles and other readings	Short speech or debate on zoo topic	Guiding metaphor: Seasons? Tree? Plant? Garden?	**Experiences** • Service learning experience involving nature, family, relationships
• P: "Silver Star," by Stafford	• C: Poem in response to "Silver Star"	Interview x people about the Big Idea question		• Speaker(s) thru Beth
• P: "Blessings," by Wright	• P: Observational writing			• Field trip or other experience (e.g., Coyote Point, zoo, other)
• P: "Death of a Naturalist," by Heaney	• RN: Response to lit			
• P: "Summer Day," by Oliver	• P: Independent reading essay at GP's end			
• P: "Tyger, Tyger," by Blake	• RN: Descriptive writing about a tree in Wash. Park			
• NF: Misc. zoo articles	• P: Final reflection on the Big Idea question			**Viewing** • pbs.org/wnet/nature/database.html
• NF: Goodall speech/article	• P: Summarize and analyze interviews about the Big Idea question			• Images in ads and other media re: man and nature
• NF: Natural world, interesting stories from news, magazines, Web				• YouTube: magical video of animals (e.g., starlings at Otmoor)
• OL: misc. websites related to quicksearch project(s)				• Al Gore: Nobel speech
• NF: "Perfect Storm"				• *Planet Earth* DVD segments
• NF: "Into Thin Air"				• *Inconvenient Truth*
• SS: "To Build a Fire"				

Additional questions to consider:

- How does nature demand respect?
- Should you live for the present or the future?
- Can where you are change who you are?
- What is our place in nature?
- What gifts does the earth provide?
- What are the different faces of nature?
- What can we learn from disaster?
- What happens when freedom vanishes?
- What are nature's mysteries?
- Are all things connected?
- What do we owe the current and future generations?
- Does beauty matter?
- How has science changed our lives?
- Do animals have rights?

Key:
G: Grammar; Voc: Vocabulary; P: Poetry; RN: Readers Notebook; C: Creative Writing; SS: Short Story; NF: Nonfiction; OL: Online

Figure 4.14

Using Essential Questions to Design Your Own Units

Some Final Thoughts

So far you have read about how I apply the instructional principles in *my* classes; now it is time to apply these ideas to *your* classes. Such units are best created through collaboration—a group of minds coming together to challenge and to help clarify different ideas. As reforms like Professional Learning Communities become more a part of the structure of the schools in which we teach, collaboration will emerge as a vital component of our work. Schmoker (2005) offers a succinct summary of such a community of learners as

> . . . a group of teachers who meet regularly as a team to identify essential and valued student learning, develop common formative assessments, analyze current levels of achievement, set achievement goals, share strategies, and then create lessons to improve upon those levels. (xii)

While the steps listed at the end of this section suggest something of an "order of operations" for designing such units, the truth is that you can begin at any number of places. Some teachers must focus everything they do on teaching a specific standard or set of standards; those teachers should just ask what ideas

and questions naturally arise and build the unit around that, choosing the texts that will best support such a sequence (see Appendix D, "Designing a Standards-Based Curriculum"). Others teach in schools where the texts and their availability drives instruction. "What's that? Oh, *Of Mice and Men* is available tomorrow for the next two weeks? I guess I will jump on that and teach it while the book is available."

In such cases teachers might simply ask which questions and concepts are central to that text and use the questions that follow to guide their planning. Whichever best describes your situation, it helps to collaborate, though this is not always possible. It is, however, increasingly possible through online communities, such as www.englishcompanion.ning.com, where English teachers can meet others and set up joint projects or get feedback on their assignments from colleagues.

We teach in an era of dramatically increased accountability, far removed from the one I encountered when I took my first job in the late 1980s; at that school I was merely given a list of titles on the first day when I asked "What should I teach?" The current emphasis on testing and measurement, accountability, and Annual Yearly Progress (AYP) threatens to reduce education and our work to a list of skills to be taught without any regard for the deeper, more meaningful content of the curriculum we came to teach. Yet I have not experienced "standards-based instruction" as an obstacle to creating engaging lessons that provide the skills and knowledge students need while also ensuring that they have the experiences we would want our own children to have in school.

In her book *Powerful Learning: What We Know About Teaching for Understanding* (2008), Linda Darling-Hammond identifies several "principles of learning for effective teaching" that are reflected in this book and the chapter you are about to use to design your own unit. Specifically, Darling-Hammond describes the following three "fundamental and well-established principles of learning that are particularly important for teaching":

1. Students come to the classroom with prior knowledge that must be addressed if teaching is to be effective. If what they know and believe is not engaged, learners may fail to grasp the new concepts and information that are taught, or they may learn them for purposes of a test but not be able to apply them elsewhere, reverting to their own preconceptions.

2. Students need to organize and use knowledge conceptually if they are to apply it beyond the classroom. To develop competence in an area of inquiry, students must not only acquire a deep foundation of factual knowledge but also understand facts and ideas in the context of a conceptual framework, and organize knowledge in ways that facilitate retrieval and application.

3. Students learn more effectively if they understand how they learn and how to manage their own learning. A "metacognitive" approach to instruction can help students learn to take control of their own learning by having a set of learning strategies, defining their own learning goals, and monitoring their progress in achieving them. (4)

To these, Darling-Hammond adds that "studies consistently find that highly effective teachers support the process of meaningful learning by":

- Creating *ambitious and meaningful tasks* that reflect how knowledge is used in the field

- Engaging students in *active learning* so that they apply and test what they know

- Drawing *connections to students' prior knowledge* and experiences

- Diagnosing student understanding in order to *scaffold the learning process* step by step

- *Assessing student learning continuously* and adapting teaching to student needs

- Providing clear *standards*, constant *feedback*, and opportunities for work

- Encouraging *strategic and metacognitive thinking* so that students can learn to evaluate and guide their own learning (5)

A full-size version of the planning list, customizable and reproducible, is available at www. heinemann.com.

Now it's time to take these ideas—those I have shared throughout this book, yours, and your colleagues'—and get to work. Use the list on the pages that follow to help you plan your own units. If you need further help, consult the Academic Essentials grid, the list of Big Questions, the Designing a Standards-Based Curriculum list, and the Unit Planning Sheet in the appendices, and/or refer to the examples I have provided throughout the book. If possible, work with others on your team, in your department, or across departments if there is room for more ambitious collaboration such as I enjoyed for years with a colleague in my school's social studies department. Good luck!

1. **Establish the Outcomes**: What should students know and be able to do by the end of this unit?	
2. **Align with Standards**: Which state standards can you most naturally incorporate into this unit? Which standards merit revisiting or reteaching (from previous units)—and how can they be effectively integrated into this unit?	
3. **Generate Concepts and Topics**: What concepts, topics, or themes would be of the most interest and create the best instructional context for your students at this time?	
4. **Determine Enduring Understandings**: What would you expect students to learn that they will remember and use in five years?	

5. **Identify Big Ideas**: List the most compelling, viable Big Ideas related to the concepts and topics you generated earlier.

6. **Develop Questions**: What compelling or essential questions do these Big Ideas invite students to consider?

7. **Incorporate the Academic Essentials**: Which of the Academic Essentials can you most effectively incorporate into this unit? How and when will you communicate these to your students?

8. **Assess Necessary Background Knowledge:** What facts, words, information, or skills will students need to know if they are to complete and learn from the assignments that comprise your unit?

9. **Evaluate Student Engagement**: Which aspects of the unit will increase and sustain the engagement of your students, particularly those often described as disaffected or underachieving?	
10. **Define Assessment Criteria:** Which criteria will you use to evaluate students' work on this unit? How and when will you communicate these criteria to your students?	
11. **Choose the Texts**: What texts will help your students most effectively explore and achieve a thorough understanding of your Big Idea and related questions? Consider looking through the textbook, if you use one, to find interesting connections across those units the publisher developed. Consider different genres: fiction, nonfiction, poetry, art, infographics, websites, articles, blogs, and so on.	
12. **Consider Supplemental Experiences:** Which of the following experiences would add value to your unit: guest speakers, field trips (actual and virtual), designing a website, creating a wiki, communicating with other students or experts via Skype, blogging, vlogging, or others.	

13. **Anticipate and Create Additional Questions:** What other questions should you expect students to come up with and/or take time to consider as part of this inquiry and in light of the texts you chose?	
14. **Assess Progress and Performance:** How will you measure students' understanding, performances, products, and progress during and after the unit? What means and evidence are most suitable for assessing this unit and this subject?	
15. **Allow a Range of Culminating Performances:** Which of the following would be appropriate culminating assignments for this particular unit: paper, multimedia presentation, graphic illustration, formal speech, visual explanation, dramatic performance, website, video, photo essay, podcast, or some combination of these?	
16. **Organize the Unit:** How should you organize the different elements of your unit? What should go first? And after that? If there is a core work, such as a novel, at the heart of the unit, when should it be read? How are the other, supplemental texts related to this core work? What is the rationale for your organizational strategy?	

17. **Differentiate Instruction:** What obstacles might undermine the success or engagement of English Learners, Special Education Students, or GATE students? What accommodations or modifications can you make to the assignment to ensure the likelihood of their success?	
18. **Identify Opportunities for Language Study:** What elements of language—vocabulary, rhetoric, grammar, usage, conventions—naturally arise in this unit? How can you best incorporate and effectively teach them?	
19. **Integrate Technology:** Which of the following technology applications would add value to and increase engagement in this assignment: social networking, blog, a wiki, videos, podcast, photography, PowerPoint, Skype, or some other technology that has come out in the time it has taken me to write this sentence?	
20. **Choose an Appropriate Configuration:** Should students work on this assignment—or portions of it—individually, in pairs, small groups, or large groups? What will these different configurations need in order to be effective?	

Of Mice and Men Chapter-by-Chapter Reading Notes and Questions
Please answer all questions on a separate page.

Of Mice and Men

Reading Notes: Chapter One (pgs. 1–16)

Introduction While reading *Of Mice and Men*, we will pause to make some observations. These observations are intended to improve your ability to see and interpret key ideas and events in the story. Write your responses to these questions on a separate sheet of paper *as you read*. It's fine to type your responses if you prefer. Responses to each question should be thorough, not just a few words or single sentence.

1. Generate a list of *five* words that describe Lenny. After making the list, choose the *one* word you think *best* describes him, then explain why, using examples from the text to support and illustrate your idea.

2. Generate a list of *five* words that describe George. After making the list, choose the *one* word you think *best* describes him, then explain why, using examples from the text to support and illustrate your idea.

3. Complete the following sentence: *The relationship between George and Lenny is like.* . . . After you complete the sentence, explain why their relationship is like *x*, then provide examples to support and illustrate your idea. Explain how these examples relate to the main idea.

4. Speculate about what happened in Weed that caused them to have to leave; and predict what you think will happen in this story based on what happened before. What details do you base your prediction on?

5. Develop two test questions based on the first chapter:

    a. **Right There (Literal) Question**: This is a factual question that you can answer by pointing "right there" on the page to find the answer. An example from *The Odyssey* would be, "What test did Odysseus pass that the suitors could not?" (Answer: Stringing his bow and shooting the arrow through a row of ax handles.)

    b. **Between the Lines (Inferential) Question**: This question is more complex. The answer cannot be pointed to on the page but must be *inferred* from other details in the story. An example from *The Odyssey* would be, "How would you characterize the relationship between Odysseus and his men?"

Of Mice and Men

Reading Notes: Chapter Two (pgs. 17–27)

Introduction While reading *Of Mice and Men* we will pause to make some observations. These observations are intended to improve your ability to see and interpret key ideas and events in the story. Write your responses to these questions on a separate sheet of paper *as you read*. It's fine to type your responses if you prefer. Responses to each question should be thorough, not just a few words or single sentence.

1. List *three* qualities of a good friend. Write down the three adjectives. A good friend is _____, _____, and _____.

2. Provide examples of each of these qualities from pages 17–27. Include the page number.

3. What animal would you say Curley is most like? (Focus on pages 24–27.) Explain by including examples and quotations from the text to support and illustrate your point.

4. Define the word *foreshadow* or *foreshadowing*. What event is *foreshadowed* on pages 26–27? What specific words support your prediction?

5. Based on the details Steinbeck uses to describe the bunkhouse (17–19), how would you characterize the lives of the men who work on the ranch? Use specific words and explain why those are the right words to describe them.

6. Develop two test questions based on the second chapter:

    a. **Right There (Literal) Question**: This is a factual question that you can answer by pointing "right there" on the page to find the answer. An example from *The Odyssey* would be, "What test did Odysseus pass that the suitors could not?" (Answer: Stringing his bow and shooting the arrow through a row of ax handles.)

    b. **Between the Lines (Inferential) Question**: This question is more complex. The answer cannot be pointed to on the page but must be *inferred* from other details in the story. An example from *The Odyssey* would be, "How would you characterize the relationship between Odysseus and his men?"

Of Mice and Men Chapter-by-Chapter Reading Notes and Questions
Please answer all questions on a separate page.

Of Mice and Men

Reading Notes: Chapter Two (pgs. 27–37)

Introduction While reading *Of Mice and Men* we will pause to make some observations. These observations are intended to improve your ability to see and interpret key ideas and events in the story. Write your responses to these questions on a separate sheet of paper *as you read*. It's fine to type your responses if you prefer. Responses to each question should be thorough, not just a few words or single sentence.

1. *Characterize:* Describe Curley's wife by focusing on her relationship with Curley and the men.

2. *Predict:* Based on what you know so far about Curley, his wife, and the men, what do you think will be the main conflict in the story?

3. *Connect:* What connections can you make between this story, your own life, the world in general, or other texts you have read? Explain them in detail.

4. *Connect:* How might you compare the relationship between Lennie and George and Candy and his old dog? (See page 36.)

5. *Infer:* On pages 27–37, the mood of the story changes. Generate several words to describe the mood in the story in the beginning and at the end of Chapter Two. What *causes* the change?

6. Develop two test questions based on the second chapter:

   a. **Right There (Literal) Question**: This is a factual question that you can answer by pointing "right there" on the page to find the answer. An example from *The Odyssey* would be, "What test did Odysseus pass that the suitors could not?" (Answer: Stringing his bow and shooting the arrow through a row of ax handles.)

   b. **Between the Lines (Inferential) Question**: This question is more complex. The answer cannot be pointed to on the page but must be *inferred* from other details in the story. An example from *The Odyssey* would be, "How would you characterize the relationship between Odysseus and his men?"

Of Mice and Men Chapter-by-Chapter Reading Notes and Questions
Please answer all questions on a separate page.

Of Mice and Men

Reading Notes: Chapter Three (pgs. 38–50)

Introduction While reading *Of Mice and Men* we will pause to make some observations. These observations are intended to improve your ability to see and interpret key ideas and events in the story. Write your responses to these questions on a separate sheet of paper *as you read.* It's fine to type your responses if you prefer. Responses to each question should be thorough, not just a few words or single sentence.

1. *Exposition:* List five *key details* that provide background to the characters and the plot up to this point. Explain why each detail is so important to the story.

2. *Rising Action*: List and describe the events in Chapter Three that increase the tension in the story and will lead to the climax. In a short paragraph, identify the events and explain *how* they affect the plot.

3. *Connect/Characterize:* Everyone respects Slim, especially Candy (p. 45) for whom "Slim's opinions were law." Write down a few reasons why people respect someone. Who is someone *you* respect, someone whose opinions are law? Explain *why* everyone respects Slim and how Slim is similar to or different from this person you respect so much.

4. *Infer:* Steinbeck includes a lot of animals in the story, including mice, rabbits, and dogs. Think about these animals and their relationship to the humans. What do you think Steinbeck is trying to say by using these animals? Why do you think that? Provide evidence to support your argument.

5. *Mood:* On pages 48–49, Steinbeck refers to "silence" repeatedly. What is the cause and meaning of the *silence*? Note that he personifies silence. Find some examples in which he personifies silence and explain how this technique affects the mood.

6. Develop two test questions based on the third chapter:
    a. **Right There (Literal) Question**: This is a factual question that you can answer by pointing "right there" on the page to find the answer. An example from *The Odyssey* would be, "What test did Odysseus pass that the suitors could not?" (Answer: Stringing his bow and shooting the arrow through a row of ax handles.) Answer the question and explain its importance.
    b. **Between the Lines (Inferential) Question**: This question is more complex. The answer cannot be pointed to on the page but must be *inferred* from other details in the story. An example from *The Odyssey* would be, "How would you characterize the relationship between Odysseus and his men?" Answer the question and explain its importance.

Of Mice and Men Chapter-by-Chapter Reading Notes and Questions
Please answer all questions on a separate page.

Of Mice and Men

Reading Notes: Chapter Three (pgs. 50–65)

Introduction While reading *Of Mice and Men* we will pause to make some observations. These observations are intended to improve your ability to see and interpret key ideas and events in the story. Write your responses to these questions on a separate sheet of paper *as you read.* It's fine to type your responses if you prefer. Responses to each question should be thorough, not just a few words or single sentence.

1. *Climax:* Which event in Chapter Three seems like it will be the climax of the story? Explain why you think that.

2. *Theme:* On pages 56–59, Lennie speaks eagerly and repeatedly about "live on the fatta the lan'" (which means "live on the fat of the land") when he thinks about the farm he and George will own one day. What does this place represent for George and Lennie? Explain why you think this, using examples and quotations to support your thinking.

3. *Connect:* Describe a place you already know or wish you had where you could escape all the troubles of the world. Be very specific in your details. *Paint* this place with words!

4. *Respond:* John Steinbeck said, "In every bit of honest writing in the world there is a base theme: Try to understand men; if you understand each other you will be kind to each other. Knowing a man well never leads to hate and nearly always leads to love." Explain what you think this quotation means and how it relates to the novel and your own experience.

5. *Predict:* You are roughly halfway through the novel. Based on what you know at this point, what do you think will happen in the remainder of the story? What do you base your prediction on?

6. Develop two test questions based on the third chapter:

    a. **Right There (Literal) Question**: This is a factual question that you can answer by pointing "right there" on the page to find the answer. An example from *The Odyssey* would be, "What test did Odysseus pass that the suitors could not?" (Answer: Stringing his bow and shooting the arrow through a row of ax handles.)

    b. **Between the Lines (Inferential) Question**: This question is more complex. The answer cannot be pointed to on the page but must be *inferred* from other details in the story. An example from *The Odyssey* would be, "How would you characterize the relationship between Odysseus and his men?"

Of Mice and Men

Reading Notes: Chapter Four (pgs. 66–83)

Introduction While reading *Of Mice and Men* we will pause to make some observations. These observations are intended to improve your ability to see and interpret key ideas and events in the story. Write your responses to these questions on a separate sheet of paper *as you read.* It's fine to type your responses if you prefer. Responses to each question should be thorough, not just a few words or single sentence.

1. *Theme:* Throughout the book Steinbeck explores human weakness, showing how one person or group dominates those who are weaker. Create a chart like the one below in your notebook and fill it in:

Strong	Verb	Weak	Reason
Person *X*	belittles	person *Y*	to prove to *Z* that he . . .
1.			
2.			
3.			
4.			

2. *Analyze:* Steinbeck suggests that many of the characters have some problem—suffer from something that sets them apart from others. Create a table like the one below in your notebook and use the same sentence structure as you make your analytical statements about four characters.

Person	Problem	Cause	Effect
Person *X*	feels *Y*	because of *Z*	which makes them do/feel *A*
1.			
2.			
3.			
4.			

3. Develop two test questions based on the fourth chapter:

   a. **Right There (Literal) Question**: This is a factual question that you can answer by pointing "right there" on the page to find the answer. An example from *The Odyssey* would be, "What test did Odysseus pass that the suitors could not?" (Answer: Stringing his bow and shooting the arrow through a row of ax handles.)

   b. **Between the Lines (Inferential) Question**: This question is more complex. The answer cannot be pointed to on the page but must be *inferred* from other details in the story. An example from *The Odyssey* would be, "How would you characterize the relationship between Odysseus and his men?"

Of Mice and Men Chapter-by-Chapter Reading Notes and Questions
Please answer all questions on a separate page.

Of Mice and Men

Reading Notes: Chapters Five and Six (pgs. 84–108)

Introduction While reading *Of Mice and Men*, we will pause to make some observations. These observations are intended to improve your ability to see and interpret key ideas and events in the story. Write your responses to the questions on this sheet in the Notes section of your Reader's Notebook *as you read*.

1. *Plot:* Draw and label a plot diagram with details from throughout the story that go with each stage.

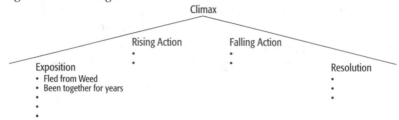

2. *Character:* Curley's wife is never given a name. Speculate about why Steinbeck refers to her as "Curley's wife." Also, generate a list of three words that describe her as a person, then choose *one* and explain why that word best characterizes her. Provide examples to support.

3. *Represent:* Think of one word that describes all the characters in the book— one word that somehow captures what they all have in common. Then write a paragraph in which you apply it to the characters and include examples that show what you mean. Here's a sample:

    > All the characters, including Curley's wife, are *x*. Curley, for example, shows he is *x* by . . . And Carlson is no different. While different from Curley, Carlson . . . Several others, Candy and Crooks, . . . Finally, Lennie and George, despite their differences, are both . . . For example, . . .

4. *Reflect and Respond:* Throughout the reading of this novel, our Big Question has been, "Am I my brother's keeper?" Now that you have finished the novel, reflect on what you think this means in general, and as it applies to the novel in particular. Include examples from the story and your experience to support your thinking.

5. *Reflect and Relate:* At the end of the story, George kills Lennie. Reflect on what he did and why he did it. In what way is killing Lennie being "his brother's keeper"? Of course, if you think this was *not* the sort of thing a "brother's keeper" does, discuss why and defend your argument with examples and details from the text and/or your experience.

THE ACADEMIC ESSENTIALS

What we need to know and be able to do if we are to succeed in the 21st century as students, workers, and citizens.	**GENERATE** • Questions • Hypotheses • Claims • Connections • Ideas • Alternatives • Categories	**EVALUATE** • Importance • Effectiveness • Relevance • Validity • Accuracy • Quality	**ANALYZE** • Cause/Effect • Problem • Implications • Logic • Consequences • Relationships • Results	**ORGANIZE** • Spatial • Cause/Effect • Chronological • Importance • Problem/Sol. • Classification • Compare/Cont.	**SYNTHESIZE** • Info/Data • Events • Ideas • Sources • Perspectives • Elements	**ASSESS** • Product • Process • Next Steps • Strategies • Alternatives
READ • Literary • Informational • Persuasive • Multimedia • Visual/Graphic						
WRITE • Explanation • Narrative • Commentary • Argument • Summary • Critique						
SPEAK & LISTEN • Discussion • Speech • Presentation • Online Discussion						
REPRESENT • Visual Explanation • Graphic Display • Dramatic Performance • Numerical Expression • Multimedia Presentation						
OBSERVE • People • Processes • Performances						
TAKE NOTES • Lecture • Research • Reading Lit/Info Text • Textbook						
TAKE TESTS • Multiple Choice • Essay • Short Answer						
	CURIOSITY	PERSISTENCE	IMAGINATION	ATTENTION	EMPATHY	PURPOSE

CRITICAL THINKING · COMMUNICATION · COLLABORATION · CONTENT

The Big Questions

from Holt McDougal Harcourt's *Literature* Series

The following questions derive from the Holt McDougal Harcourt *Literature* program, for which I served as a senior consultant. We organized around these questions to be consistent with findings about inquiry from other program senior consultants: Arthur Applebee, Judith Langer, Carol Booth Olson, Robert Marzano, Carol Ann Tomlinson, Janet Allen, Yvette Jackson, and Donna Ogle.

While these questions are used to guide instruction and organize units, you might also use them as the basis for class discussions, writing topics, speech topics, or project ideas. Also, the grade levels correlate with the units in the *Literature* program, but the questions can be used at any level.

Grade 6

What do you fear most?

Can first impressions be trusted?

What if your whole world changed?

How powerful is loyalty?

Does nature demand respect?

When is there strength in numbers?

Have you ever been fooled?

Who would you be if you could be someone else?

Is age more than a number?

What makes a hero?

How do you deal with a bully?

What would you do for your family?

What is a character's true identity?

What makes a perfect Saturday?

What happens when freedom vanishes?

How do we know we're grown up?

What would you risk for someone else?

Can memories keep the past alive?

When is a trip an adventure?

Should you live for the present or the future?

How do possibilities become reality?

Can how you look change who you are?

Are people more alike or different?

Are there two sides to every story?

When is a story a treasure?

What builds confidence?

How strong is peer pressure?

When are words not enough?

When is logic not logical?

What gives an artist style?

Why do we love sports?

When is your work your life?

What are nature's mysteries?

How much can one word say?

How do you see the world?

When do attitudes need adjusting?

Can language surprise you?

When is food more than fuel?

How powerful is love?

Can pride ever hurt you?

Is fear ever fun?

What is true friendship?

Why do we exaggerate?

When is it time to let go?

Is goodness always rewarded?
Why attempt the impossible?
Do we have to accept our limits?
Can you believe your eyes?
How do you unlock a mystery?
How would you like to be remembered?
Are monsters real?

How smart are animals?
How can we uncover the past?
What's the full news story?
Can a game play you?
Can we ever tame what's wild?
What good comes from a good deed?
How do you capture a customer?

Grade 7

How do you make a good impression?
Why are pets good companions?
Who sees the best in you?
What makes you brave?
What can we learn from disasters?
When do you feel most alive?
Do sports fans care too much?
What turns a crowd into a mob?
What makes your imagination soar?
What has the power to heal?
What stands in the way of your dreams?
Who deserves a second chance?
Why do people misbehave?
What if you could meet your hero?
What do you need to survive?
What do we learn from our elders?
What happens when friends compete?
What makes a community?
What is the cure for unhappiness?
What makes a gift special?
Can you be alone and not lonely?
How important is money?
What's the message?
Can where you are change who you are?
Is it brave to suffer in silence?
Where do people find hope?
What makes us laugh?
Does everyone love being in love?
Are all things connected?
When is a photo more than a picture?

Why do we need memorials?
What is our place in nature?
Whom do you feel closest to?
What is honor?
How do the seasons affect you?
When does nonsense make sense?
How would you describe yourself?
Do you think before you act?
Should people always reach for the stars?
Is there a job you were born to do?
Is chivalry dead?
What can we learn from stories?
What makes a good couple?
Would you rather be clever or strong?
What is your duty to others?
What does your name really mean?
What is a winner?
When is there dignity in silence?
What makes a person a trailblazer?
How can we change what's wrong?
Why should you keep trying?
Can appearances deceive?
Can you tell fact from fiction?
How do we fight disease?
What decisions shape the news?
Are people paid fairly?
Do we have our priorities straight?
What inspires people?
How do you sell an idea?

Grade 8

What's worth the effort?	Can films make history fresh?
Is any plan foolproof?	How can words create pictures?
When does trash become treasure?	What's the smartest animal?
What makes you suspicious?	Does beauty matter?
Is seeing believing?	Can you be rich without money?
How do great stories begin?	What is good advice?
When is it time to leave?	When does form matter?
When is it OK to be scared?	When do you feel most free?
When does truth become legend?	When do poems tell a story?
What do you cherish?	Who is the real you?
When is it better not to know?	How do you make decisions?
Can allies be opponents?	Why do we exaggerate?
What shows others who we are?	What's really normal?
What puts a character in focus?	What is the cost of victory?
When is a risk worth taking?	What makes a pioneer?
What are the signs of greatness?	Where do we get our values?
Is it ever right to give up?	How do you know what's right?
Does every contribution count?	What is a folk hero?
How do you find your purpose?	What can you learn from a job?
Are you superstitious?	What makes you proud?
Can you belong in two places?	Can cartoons have a point?
What is the role of a witness?	How can we fight injustice?
What gifts does the earth provide?	What is your dream job?
What makes something priceless?	Why do people seek danger?
Is curiosity a gift or a curse?	What's the source?
How well do we treat our elders?	What does music say about us?
What gives meaning to simple things?	Why do we sing?
What impact will you have on the world?	How has science changed our lives?

Grade 9

Would you visit the past if you could?	What sends a chill down your spine?
What does it take to be a survivor?	Are you a perfectionist?
What is a generation gap?	How important is status?
What are you willing to sacrifice?	What makes someone remarkable?
What is worth fighting for?	What is a teacher?
What makes a winner?	When is strength more than muscle?
Why are we fascinated by the unknown?	What makes a memory?

What is dignity?

What do you look for in a friend?

When is a risk worth taking?

Is revenge ever justified?

What makes a setting sinister?

Where do you find adventure?

What are the different faces of nature?

What if life had a reset button?

Why do we hurt the ones we love?

What are you really good at?

What does a community owe its children?

Where do you go to get away from it all?

How do expectations affect performance?

What place do you call home?

What is the source of inspiration?

How do scientists unlock the past?

How far would you go to find freedom?

How do you get the news?

How should you treat a guest?

What stories will you tell your children?

Can a dream change the world?

How do you sell an idea?

Is privacy an illusion?

How do you promote a cause?

Could we live without television?

Who lives in your memory?

Can you think out of the box?

What makes a great competitor?

What makes your imagination soar?

What triggers a sense of alarm?

Do you set your own course?

Is fear our worst enemy?

Are diamonds really a girl's best friend?

What makes a director a master of style?

Have you ever felt out of place?

Is "cute" a compliment?

What is a poet's job?

What would win your heart?

Who makes you laugh?

Grade 10

What if everyone were the same?

What makes something valuable?

What do you take for granted?

Should you trust your instincts?

Is survival a matter of chance?

How can we achieve the impossible?

What keeps you on the edge of your seat?

What makes you feel like an outsider?

Is there a cure for grief?

How good are you at judging people?

How important is telling the truth?

Who has made you a better person?

Are old ways the best ways?

How do you show you care?

Why do people argue over silly things?

What makes a character believable?

Does knowledge come at a price?

Is technology taking over?

What makes someone popular?

Can you recover from tragedy?

Can ordinary people be heroes?

Can you be from two cultures at once?

What's wrong with holding a grudge?

What would you do for a friend?

When do world conflicts affect us?

Who are the victims of war?

How accepting are you?

What if you had to flee your country?

When are little things a big deal?

Can beauty be captured in words?

What can we learn from disaster?

Is the news always reliable?

Can reporters always stay objective?
What do we owe others?
Why keep what is no longer useful?
What would make the world safer?
Do animals have rights?
Do the ends justify the means?
What would you sacrifice for justice?
How important is wealth?
How do candidates get your vote?
What is our place in nature?
What if you couldn't fail?
What animal reminds you of yourself?
Which memories last?
What makes a good love poem?
When does poetry sing?
What breeds terror?
What do we learn from experience?

How can nature inspire you?
Can you paint a picture with words?
What is your role in your household?
What if your government declared you the enemy?
How can we change society?
Whose life is it, anyway?
What is cowardice?
How does it feel to start over?
What are the signs of the times?
What is your ultimate loyalty?
Could you be a knight?
Do heroes get to be human?
Why do we admire dreamers?
Can your conscience mislead you?
What gives a scene its power?

American Literature

Who owns the land?
What makes an explorer?
Are people basically good?
Who has the right to rule?
Is the price of progress ever too high?
Is it patriotic to protest one's government?
Does everyone have a "dark side"?
Where do people look for truth?
What divides a nation?
Is anything worth dying for?
Why do people break rules?
Is it important to face reality?

What makes a place unique?
Does the universe care?
How are women's roles changing?
Why are there "haves" and "have nots"?
What is modern?
Can ideals survive catastrophe?
How can people honor their heritage?
What drives human behavior?
Are we responsible for the whole world?
Can America achieve equal rights?
What makes an American?
What is the American?

British Literature

What makes a true hero?
Who really shapes society?
Does fate control our lives?
Can people live up to high ideals?
Should religion be tied to politics?

Why is love so complicated?
What is the ideal society?
Why do people seek power?
What can fix society's problems?
Can science tell us how to live?

What topics are newsworthy?
What is a woman's role in public life?
What can people learn from nature?
Is emotion stronger than reason?
When is the ordinary extraordinary?
How does war change our values?
When is progress a problem?

Can values be imposed?
Is it better to escape or face reality?
Why do people fear change?
What does it mean to be modern?
Are we all alone?
How important is culture?
Why is there always war?

Designing a Standards-Based Curriculum

BEFORE: Instructional Design

Effective instruction requires a purpose and meaningful context that etablishes not only what but why students must learn the assigned materials. Rationales such as "to meet the standards" or "to pass the test" lack meaning and do not motivate.

- **CONTENT STANDARDS** *What should students know and be able to do by the end of this task, unit, or course?*

  ### Considerations

  Connections to previous and future skills and concepts

  Constraints of time and recources

  Availability of necessary materials and resources

- **STUDENT PREPARATION** *What should students know and be able to do to accomplish Content Standards goals?*

  ### Considerations

  Specialized or new vocabulary terms

  Background knowledge on the idea, historical period, or story

  Skills, habits, capacities, or techniques

  Connections to previously learned skills and concepts

- **TEACHER PREPARATION** *What skills, knowledge, or resources does the teacher need to effectively teach this skill or concept?*

  ### Considerations

  What the teacher needs or wants to teach after this unit

  What support or material resources are available to help teach this skill or concept?

- **INSTRUCTIONAL STANDARDS** *What strategies and instructional designs are most effective and efficient in teaching this skill or concept?*

Considerations

Graphic organizers

Note-taking strategies

Instructional strategies: reciprocal teaching, literature circles, direct instruction

Class and student configurations (e.g., pairs, groups, whole class)

Visual aids, multimodal, multisensory approaches

- **CURRICULAR CONVERSATIONS** *How does this skill or concept relate to the larger themes in the course, curriculum, or lives of students?*

Considerations

Workplace connections

Personal connections

Cross-curricular connections

- **STANDARDS ALIGNMENT** *Which standard(s) will this task or unit help students master?*

Considerations

Curricular objectives and context of the lesson

Current progress toward mastery of this standard

Connections to and reinforcement of standards students have already met

Standards you have not yet addressed or which students have not yet mastered

Extent to which this task or unit prepares students to meet other standards, for example, district frameworks, ESLRs, Advanced Placement, exit exam, or SAT standards

- **PERFORMANCE STANDARDS** *What evidence of student learning or mastery are you willing to accept?*

Considerations

Is there more than one way to show mastery of this skill or concept?

Do students have ample opportunity and means by which to master this standard?

Do students know what a successful performance looks like (e.g., through exemplars or modeling)?

Do students know the criteria by which their performance will be evaluated up front (e.g., through exemplars, rubrics, directions, modeling)?

Are the criteria for mastery consistent with those in other classes, schools, districts, and states?

Are all skills and concepts equally important—and given equal weight—on all assessments?

Is this method an effective and appropriate use of the teacher's time and attention?

DURING: Implementation and Experience

Effective design demands that we lay a solid but adaptable foundation that will ensure the success of the task or unit once it begins. While such attention to design asks a lot of the teacher at first, such questions and considerations become mental habits that lead to efficient and effective instructional design.

- **TEACHING AND LEARNING** *This list offers a sequence of steps that build on learners' knowledge and progress by extending their capacity and competence as they move toward mastery of a standard:*

Considerations

Introduce the skill, concept, or task with clear instructions that students can hear, see, and read.

Connect the task, concept, or unit to what they have studied or will study.

Assess prior knowledge and current understanding of the skill or concept.

Demonstrate the task, explaining what you are thinking as you do so.

Try the task or explain their initial understanding of the concept.

Evaluate their performance; check for understanding.

Correct or clarify their performance as needed, based on observed results.

Practice the skill or continue study of the concept.

Assess level of mastery and need for further group or individualized instruction.

Extend students' understanding and mastery by increasing the difficulty of the task.

Monitor students' level of mastery and need for further group or individualized instruction.

Reinforce understanding and mastery as you move on to next task or concept.

AFTER: Evaluation and Planning

Feedback and reinforcement are essential elements in any instructional design. In this last stage, teachers answer the question "What next?" before returning to the beginning and starting the process with a new task or concept.

- **INSTRUCTIONAL STANDARDS** *What does the performance data tell you the students need to do or learn next?*

Considerations

Did all students master the skill or concept?

What is the next step—and why?

Was your method the most effective means to teach this skill or concept?

What changes should you make in the technique or assignment next time?

- **WHAT'S NEXT** *Return to the beginning and follow the sequence for teaching the next skill or concept.*

Unit Plan: _____

Big Idea					
Reading	**Writing**	**Speaking**	**Investigations**	**Misc.**	
				Language Study	
				Experiences	
				Viewing	

Additional questions to consider:

Adler, Mortimer. 1982. *The Paideia Proposal: An Educational Manifesto.* New York: Touchstone.

Applebee, Arthur. 1996. *Curriculum as Conversation: Transforming Traditions of Teaching and Learning.* Chicago: University of Chicago Press.

Atwell, Nancie. 2007. *The Reading Zone: How to Help Kids Become Skilled, Passionate, Habitual, Critical Readers.* New York: Scholastic.

Bauerline, Mark. 2008. *The Dumbest Generation: How the Digital Age Stupefies Young Americans and Jeopardizes Our Future.* New York: Tarcher/Penguin.

Burke, Jim. 2007. *Academic Workout: Reading and Language Arts.* North Billerica, MA: Curriculum Associates.

Christensen, Linda. 2000. *Reading, Writing, and Rising Up: Teaching About Social Justice and the Power of the Written Word.* Milwaukee: Rethinking Schools.

Copeland, Matt. 2005. *Socratic Circles: Fostering Critical and Creative Thinking in Middle and High School.* Portland, ME: Stenhouse.

Costa, Arthur, and Ballick, Bena. 2000. *Habits of Mind,* ed. Arthur Costa and Bena Ballick. Alexandria, VA: Association for Supervision and Curriculum Development.

Covey, Stephen R. 1989. *The Seven Habits of Highly Effective People.* New York: Simon and Schuster.

Cushman, Kathleen. 1989. "Asking the Essential Questions: Curriculum Development." *HORACE,* Vol 5. No. 5, p. 2.

Damon, William. 2008. *The Path to Purpose: Helping Our Children Find Their Calling in Life.* New York: Free Press.

Darling-Hammond, Linda. 2008. *Powerful Learning: What We Know About Teaching for Understanding.* San Francisco: Jossey-Bass.

Fadem, Terry J. 2009. *The Art of Asking: Ask Better Questions, Get Better Answers.* Upper Saddle River, NJ: Pearson.

Friedman, Thomas L. 2006. *The World Is Flat: A Brief History of the Twenty-First Century.* New York: Farrar, Straus and Giroux.

Gardner, Howard. 2000. *The Disciplined Mind: What All Students Should Understand.* New York: Simon and Schuster.

———. 2006. *Five Minds for the Future.* Cambridge: Harvard Business School Press.

Gardner, Walt. 2008. "From Feds on Down, AP Students Are Being Neglected." *Seattle Post-Intelligencer.* http://seattlepoi.nwsource.com/opinion/346155_focuseducation06.html. Accessed on July 10.

Golden, John. 2001. *Reading in the Dark: Using Film as a Tool in the English Classroom.* Urbana, IL: National Council of Teachers of English.

Guthrie, John T., and Wigfield, Allan. 1997. *Reading Engagement: Motivating Readers Through Integrated Instruction.* Newark, DE: International Reading Association.

Hyerle, David. 1996. *Visual Tools: For Constructing Knowledge*. Alexandria, VA: Association for Supervision and Curriculum Development.

Intersegmental Committee of the Academic Senates (ICAS). 2000. *Academic Literacy: A Statement of Competencies Expected of Students Entering California's Public Colleges and Universities*. Sacramento: ICAS.

Intrator, Sam M. 2005. *Tuned in and Fired Up: How Teaching Can Inspire Real Learning in the Classroom*. New Haven: Yale University Press.

Ivey, Gay, and Fisher, Douglas. 2006. *Creating Literacy-Rich Schools for Adolescents*. Alexandria, VA: Association for Supervision and Curriculum Development.

Jackson, Maggie. 2008. *Distracted: The Erosion of Attention and the Coming Dark Age*. Amherst, NY: Prometheus.

Jackson, Yvette, and Cooper, Eric J. 2007. "Building Academic Success with Underachieving Adolescents." In *Adolescent Literacy: Turning Promise into Practice*, eds. Kylene Beers, Robert E. Probst, and Linda Rief. Portsmouth, NH: Heinemann.

Jensen, Eric. 2005. *Teaching with the Brain in Mind*. Alexandria, VA: Association for Supervision and Curriculum Development.

Langer, Judith. 2002. *Effective Literacy Instruction: Building Successful Reading and Writing Programs*. Urbana, IL: National Council of Teachers of English.

Light, Richard. 2004. *Making the Most of College: Students Speak Their Minds*. Cambridge: Harvard University Press.

Marinoff, Lou. 2003. *The Big Questions: How Philosophy Can Change Your Life*. New York: Bloomsbury.

Marzano, Robert J., Pickering, Debra J., and Pollock, Jane E. 2001. *Classroom Instruction that Works: Research-Based Strategies for Increasing Student Achievement*. Alexandria, VA: Association for Supervision and Curriculum Development.

National Council on Education and the Economy (NCEE). 2007. *Touch Choices or Tough Times: The Report of the* New *Commission on the Skills of the American Workforce*. San Francisco: Wiley.

Nystrand, Martin. 2006. "Research on the Role of Classroom Discourse as It Affects Reading Comprehension." *Research on the Teaching of English*, Vol. 40, No. 4, 392–412.

Partnership for 21st Century Skills. 2008. "21st Century Skills Map." Washington, D.C.: Partnership for 21st Century Skills, National Council of Teachers of English. Accessed on April 3, 2009; www.21stcenturyskills.org/documents/english_in_black__white.pdf.

Phillips, Christopher. 2004. *Six Questions of Socrates: A Modern-Day Journey of Discovery Through World Philosophy*. New York: W. W. Norton.

Pink, Daniel. 2006. *A Whole New Mind: Why Right-Brainers Will Rule the Future*. New York: Riverhead.

Schmoker, Mike. 2005. "Here and Now: Improving and Teaching and Learning." *On Common Ground: The Power of Professional Learning Communities*, eds. Richard DuFour, Robert Eaker, and Rebecca DuFour. Bloomington, IN: Solution Tree.

Sizer, Theodore R. 1985. *Horace's Compromise: The Dilemma of the American High School.* Boston: Houghton Mifflin.

Smith, Michael W., and Wilhelm, Jeffrey D. 2002. *"Reading Don't Fix No Chevys": Literacy in the Lives of Young Men.* Portsmouth, NH: Heinemann.

Sternberg, Robert J., and Grigorenko, Elena J. 2007. *Teaching for Successful Intelligence: To Increase Student Learning and Achievement.* Thousand Oaks, CA: Corwin.

Tatum, Alfred. 2005. *Teaching Reading to Black Adolescent Males: Closing the Achievement Gap.* Portland, ME: Stenhouse.

Vygotsky, Lev. 1986. *Thought and Language.* Cambridge: MIT Press.

Washington, Denzel. 2006. *A Hand to Guide Me: Legendary Leaders Celebrate the Lives of Those Who Shaped Them.* New York: Meredith Books.

Wiggins, Grant, and McTighe, Jay. 2005. *Understanding by Design.* Alexandria, VA: Association for Supervision and Curriculum Development.

Wilhelm, Jeffrey D. 2007. *Engaging Readers and Writers with Inquiry: Promoting Deep Understandings in Language Arts and the Content Areas with Guiding Questions.* New York: Scholastic.

Willis, Judy. 2006. *Research-Based Strategies to Ignite Student Learning.* Alexandria, VA: Association for Supervision and Curriculum Development.

Zakaria, Fareed. 2008. *The Post-American World.* New York: W. W. Norton.

What's the Big Idea?

Question-Driven Units that Develop Motivated Reading, Writing, and Thinking Study Guide

Why Do Questions Matter in Curriculum? An Introduction

Engagement, understanding, and memory—three areas of urgent and growing concern for all middle and high school English teachers. How can we create a curriculum and individual lessons that not only teach the academic literacies students need to succeed in school but also those critical literacies required by the adult world and world of work in the 21st century? This section introduces the rationale and research to support the use of questions as your curriculum. After discussing what secondary and postsecondary schooling expects of students, we consider the new skills all students must cultivate if they are to succeed in the new era. Within the introduction you will find specific tools to help you develop such questions for both daily lessons and larger curricular units. This section serves to frame the core principles that I illustrate and articulate through detailed classroom examples throughout the units.

BEFORE (prior to reading the unit)

1. Why do *you* think "questions matter as curriculum"? Another way we might frame this question is to use a variation on one of my favorite questions: What is the problem for which questions are the solution?

2. Jot down a list of a few questions you find consistently engage students and enhance their ability to learn the material you teach.

3. Reflect on the list of questions you just made and identify those qualities that make them such effective, compelling questions.

4. Generate a list of questions and concerns you have about using "questions as curriculum" and briefly discuss the source and implications of those concerns.

DURING (as you read the unit)

1. Examine the "habits of mind" outlined early in the introduction. Reflect on and discuss professors' perspectives as well as your own.

2. Respond to the different perspectives on 21st-century literacy as they relate to the workplace, classroom, and society in general. How do you incorporate these ways of working and thinking into your curriculum?

3. Consider Gardener's "five minds" and Damon's work on purpose as discussed in the introduction; note that they have worked together on related projects and concerns (see *Good Work: When Excellence and Ethics Meet* by Gardner, Csikszentmihalyi, and Damon, Basic Books, 2002). How might you connect their work, as discussed in this introduction, to your department, classroom, and students?

4. Evaluate your own curriculum in terms of the types of questions you and your students ask, using those questions in Figures 1.1 and 1.2 as well as the list of Big Questions included in Appendix C.

AFTER (when you finish the unit)

1. Revisit your earlier thoughts about questions (before you read this unit). What new insights, ideas, or questions have arisen after reading it?

2. Consider the various arguments—by Applebee, Langer, Wiggins, Tatum, and Sizer—toward the end of the unit for organizing your curriculum around questions. What is their central, unifying argument? Is it possible to teach using such questions despite the pressure to address state standards and prepare students for standardized exams? The rest of the book will argue that it is not only possible but also essential that we do this. What are your thoughts?

3. What enduring questions or concerns do you have about the notion of using questions as curriculum after reading this first unit?

Sample Unit 1: An Intellectual Rite of Passage
Engaging Students with Essential Questions

We often discuss the need for young adults to participate in rites of passage, but outside of culturally prescribed rituals we ignore these important experiences. At

the heart of the educational process is change, a process whereby one discovers what they know (or want to learn more about) and can do (or want to learn to do much better). This unit looks at a semester-long project that allows students to investigate a subject of great personal interest while at the same time doing the work required by the district and other agencies (e.g., AP program) in preparation for the culminating exams at year's end. Designing such intellectual rites of passage requires long-range, big picture thinking and planning, which this unit goes into in some detail. It is organized around one Personal Inquiry Project, in this case assigned to senior AP students; I should add, however, that I have done variations on this same assignment with students at all grade and ability levels, as subsequent units about my freshman class will show.

BEFORE (prior to reading the unit)

1. Identify those projects or assignments you do that might serve as "intellectual rites of passage." What do the units do and what is your rationale for them? What is your measure of the success and effectiveness of these units?

2. What are your biggest concerns about and frustrations with students, especially seniors, during second semester?

3. What do you want students leaving your class at year's end thinking and feeling about the work they did in your class? What specific words do you want them to use when they describe your class and the work they did there? Why these words—and what do you do to accomplish that end?

DURING (as you read the unit)

1. Respond to and discuss the "backward design" questions from Wiggins and McTighe at the beginning of Unit One. To what extent does their three-stage process of design describe your own curricular designs?

2. Analyze and discuss the actual design of the Inquiry Project assignment as it appears in the unit. What surprises and concerns you the most about such a unit?

3. Notice throughout the unit that I consistently provide examples or demonstrate for students, even in advanced classes, what a successful performance looks like. What role does modeling and the use of examples play in your own class when trying to help students perform at higher levels?

AFTER (when you finish the unit)

1. Discuss the meaning and implications of a "culture of inquiry" as represented in this unit. You see students engaged in inquiry about big ideas, summer reading, and core texts, such as *Hamlet*, during which they formulate many questions about the texts. Who asks—and answers—the questions in your class?

2. Review your own (or your department's) summer reading requirement and subsequent assignments. Note that my sample summer reading assignment here is organized around pairs of books about a common topic. Compare it to your own summer reading assignment (or independent reading during the year): Which one do you prefer—and why?

Sample Unit 2: Spirited Inquiry
Creating Questions to Access a Challenging Text

This unit looks at how to use questions to teach literature, in this case *Crime and Punishment*. Even though you may not teach this particular novel, the more important point is how to use questions to teach such complex books in ways that all students can enjoy and learn from them. The unit not only looks at the use of questions as a means of inquiry for an entire work but also as a method for holding students accountable and getting them to think about the work on a more daily level. It serves as a case study of this unit, taking you through all of it from start to finish, then concluding with students' reflections on the unit and what they learned from it.

BEFORE (prior to reading the unit)

1. What makes a text or unit difficult? How do these make a text or a task difficult?

2. Respond to the epigraph by Philip Roth: What do *you* think literature should be "used" for?

3. How are your instructional units (aka your curriculum) currently organized for your class?

4. List the texts you teach and the question(s) each book invites you and your students to explore; for example, *Lord of the Flies* might invite you to consider, among others, the question, "What are we capable of?"

DURING (as you read the unit)

1. Discuss whether creativity, innovation, or intelligence can be taught or otherwise developed. On what do you base your response?

2. Choose one book (my chosen text is *Crime and Punishment*) and, using my example in Figure 2.1, generate a list of six to ten topics students could focus on throughout the book. Note that while some topics in a book might be interesting and even important, not all run throughout an entire book—an important quality of this assignment.

3. Discuss the advantages and disadvantages, your questions and concerns about using online discussion groups with students to explore these questions within a unit.

4. Explain the role discussion plays in general in your class. How do you use and configure it? What is your role during such discussions? What is the problem for which discussion—in class or online—is the solution?

AFTER (when you finish the unit)

1. Respond to the final project (Figure 2.10): What thoughts do you have about such a project in your class? How might you adapt it to better meet the needs of your own students or the culture of your school?

2. Describe the role that reflection plays in your classroom. How do you use the information to improve your instruction on the unit?

3. Discuss the content of this unit in light of the concerns and questions you had before reading the unit about using inquiry-based instruction.

4. Identify the most important or useful idea you take from this unit as it relates to your own teaching.

Sample Unit 3: Natural Curiosity
Using Questions to Explore Relationships

This unit focuses on creating a culture of high expectations for all students that is both intellectually challenging and personally meaningful. It looks at the ways we can use different tools and techniques to help all students do this more

sophisticated work, focusing here on both *Romeo and Juliet* and their own personal choice reading books to show how to apply these ideas in a range of instructional contexts.

BEFORE (prior to reading the unit)

1. Discuss the role and importance of curiosity in your class.

2. Describe the qualities of good questions and how to use them for maximum instructional effect.

3. List the intellectual and academic skills students need to do the work in your class and discuss how you incorporate them into your curriculum.

DURING (as you read the unit)

1. Review the National Center on Education and the Economy (NCEE) report on page 75: What are the implications of these for your instruction and curriculum?

2. Note that throughout the unit—and the book in general—you see students using different tools and technologies to explore topics and to help them think about complex ideas. Which tools and technologies do you have your students use to think critically and creatively? How do you *use* those tools to achieve the best instructional results?

3. Consider the importance of choice—of texts, tasks, topics—as illustrated throughout the unit. What choices do students have in your own class?

AFTER (when you finish the unit)

1. Discuss your own expectations regarding student performance in light of what you read here. Thinking of your own students, in other words, do you feel you expect more, less, or something different from your students? Explain.

2. Provide an honest answer to the question: Do you believe all students can learn what you teach and succeed, in some meaningful sense, in your class? What must they—and *you*—do to achieve this result?

3. What questions and concerns do you have after reading this unit?

4. What is missing from the instructional landscape I describe here that you feel is essential to an effective and legitimate English curriculum?

Sample Unit 4: Meaningful Conversations
Essential Questions as a Way into Required Text

This unit offers a case study of an entire unit for a novel in a freshman English class. The emphasis here is on organizing the study of required literature—*Of Mice and Men*, in this case—around meaningful questions such as "Am I my brother's keeper?" This unit shows how to use a range of media and instructional approaches in a highly interactive but challenging classroom.

BEFORE (prior to reading the unit)

1. List the "essential conversations" you think adolescents need to discuss and think about with greater depth.

2. Generate several metaphor(s) that describe your role as a teacher, especially when it comes to "meaningful conversations."

3. Discuss your thoughts about the literary canon, cultural literacy, and the Great Books concept.

4. Share your thoughts about the use of textbooks in the classroom: Do you use one? What do you like and dislike, think is effective and ineffective about the textbook you use?

DURING (as you read the unit)

1. Identify the required books you must teach. Generate a list of possible supplementary texts to examine in conjunction: fiction, nonfiction, poetry, art, film, websites, experiences, speakers, and so on.

2. Evaluate the Academic Essentials outlined in this unit and consider how you do or might apply those to your own class.

3. Compare the study guide questions and format to your own approach: What are the differences and similarities, strengths and weaknesses of each?

4. Discuss the use of blogging in the context of this assignment and how it, or some other social medium, might be used effectively in your class.

AFTER (when you finish the unit)

1. Use the Unit Plan template in Appendix E to plan or analyze your own unit around a big idea.

2. What questions and concerns remain after reading this unit?

Using Essential Questions to Design Your Own Units: Some Final Thoughts

Unit Study Intro

I have tried throughout to articulate and illustrate the principles outlined in this book. In the end, however, what matters most is that you can take these concepts and examples from my class and use them to design and implement units within your own class. The following questions invite you to think about how to make these connections while also asking you to further examine your own thoughts about instructional design.

1. Respond to Schmoker's definition of a community of learners at the begin ning of the unit. How does this compare with your classroom or vision of teaching?

2. Discuss Darling-Hammond's three principles of learning and the list of actions that follow (see pp. 156–7). How do these accord with—or differ from—your principles of teaching?

3. Reflect on the unit you created using the guidelines in the final unit. What are you trying to achieve? How is this similar to or different from the units you would normally create for your classes?